HOW TO SU[R]

ANCI[E]T

ROME

For Samuel and Patrick, as proof that Romans aren't boring.

HOW TO SURVIVE IN
ANCIENT ROME

L J TRAFFORD

PEN & SWORD
HISTORY

AN IMPRINT OF PEN & SWORD BOOKS LTD.
YORKSHIRE – PHILADELPHIA

First published in Great Britain in 2020 by
PEN AND SWORD HISTORY
An imprint of
Pen & Sword Books Ltd
Yorkshire – Philadelphia

ISBN 978 1 52675 786 9

Typeset in Times New Roman 11.5/14 by
SJmagic DESIGN SERVICES, India.
Printed and bound by CPI Group (UK) Ltd, Croydon, CR0 4YY

Pen & Sword Books Limited incorporates the imprints of Atlas, Archaeology,
Aviation, Discovery, Family History, Fiction, History, Maritime, Military, Military
Classics, Politics, Select, Transport, True Crime, Air World, Frontline Publishing,
Leo Cooper, Remember When, Seaforth Publishing, The Praetorian Press,
Wharncliffe Local History, Wharncliffe Transport, Wharncliffe True Crime and
White Owl.

For a complete list of Pen & Sword titles please contact
PEN & SWORD BOOKS LIMITED
47 Church Street, Barnsley, South Yorkshire, S70 2AS, England
E-mail: enquiries@pen-and-sword.co.uk
Website: www.pen-and-sword.co.uk

Or

PEN AND SWORD BOOKS
1950 Lawrence Rd, Havertown, PA 19083, USA
E-mail: Uspen-and-sword@casematepublishers.com
Website: www.penandswordbooks.com

Contents

Contents

List of Illustrations

22 Reconstruction of Roman weaponry. (Rolf Krahl, CC BY-SA 2.0 https://creativecommons.org/licenses/by-sa/2.0)

23 Ivory statue of Apollo, Roman, 200 BCE-300 CE. (Science Museum, London. CC BY)

24 Terracotta votive scalp, Roman, 200 BCE-200 CE. (Science Museum, London. CC BY)

25 Cornelia, the Vestal Virgin, entombed alive surrounded by bones in the dungeon. (Line engraving by G. Mochetti after B. Pinelli. Wellcome Collection. CC BY)

26 Ancient Roman silver denarius coin of Emperor. (Domitian/ Shutterstock)

27 Detail of Cicero marble statue in front of Rome Old Palace of Justice. (Shutterstock)

28 Graeco-Roman bronze phallic pendant. (Wellcome Collection. CC BY)

29 Graeco-Roman surgical instruments. (Wellcome Collection. CC BY)

Ajax and Hortensia images both by Carol Klio Burrell.

Welcome to Ancient Rome

So, you think you know ancient Rome? After all, you've seen *Gladiator* six times, you can use 'Et tu Brute' wittily in conversation and you can pepper political debate with tales of crazy Caligula making his horse a senator.

Except that you don't. Caesar never said 'Et tu Brute', Caligula never made his horse a senator, and Commodus definitely didn't meet his end at the hands of a hunky gladiator with an attractively growly voice. Commodus was murdered by a wrestler named Narcissus, who'd been set the task by the empress, after the emperor had vomited up the poisoned beef she'd served him. Proof that fact is indeed stranger than fiction.

Ancient Rome is a pretty strange place: clothes are washed in wee, babies are left in the rubbish and bad luck can be averted by wearing penis jewellery. But don't panic. We are here to guide you through this strange new world. We shall provide you with practical advice that will

prevent you from accidentally insulting the locals, committing social faux pas of an embarrassing nature and help you avoid being sewn up in a sack with a snake, a dog and a rooster.[1]

Along the way you will meet our two experts: Titus Flavius Ajax and Hortensia. Titus Flavius Ajax is a former imperial slave and now secretary to his Imperial Majesty, the emperor. He will be providing all the information you need to know on all matters imperial and all the top gossip from the palace. Hortensia is a lady of (mostly) leisure. As a member of Rome's elite class Hortensia has everything you've always wanted to know about the ultra-rich but were too afraid to ask. She also has the inside line on what it's like to be female in the Roman Empire.

Romans are enormously proud of being Roman. As Pliny the Elder says: 'Undoubtedly the one race of outstanding virtue in the whole world is the Roman'.[2] To fit in successfully with your new surroundings some knowledge of the history of this great city is required. So, recline on your couch, have a glass of fine Falerian[3] wine, nibble on a roasted dormouse, and relax as we take you on a tour of 800 years of history.

The History of Rome: The Basics

Rome's story can be roughly broken down into three parts: the Kings, the Republic and the Empire.

Before the Kings

Before there were kings of Rome and before there was Rome even, there was Aeneas. Aeneas was a hero of the Trojan War (yes, the one with the wooden horse) who, fleeing the destruction of his home city, underwent many adventures and trials, eventually ending up in Italy.

Aeneas settled himself within spitting distance of where Rome would stand, somehow never spotting that it was the perfect location for founding a city. Instead he went about founding a dynasty of kings, none of whom mustered the energy to build Rome.[4]

The Kings

Dates 753 BCE–509 BCE (approximately).

The first king of Rome was Romulus. The story of how he came to found the city is familiar to every man, woman, child and slave in Rome. To fit in successfully you too will need some familiarity with this tale, if only to avoid embarrassing yourself asking: 'Hey, what's with all those statues of those babies suckling from that dog?'

The descendants of Aeneas had been ruling a part of Italy that was very close to the site of Rome – but did not include Rome – as the kings of Alba. In the eighth century BCE King Amulius set about securing his throne by killing all of his male relatives. This was exhausting work and to save himself the effort of having to kill any more, he forced his niece,

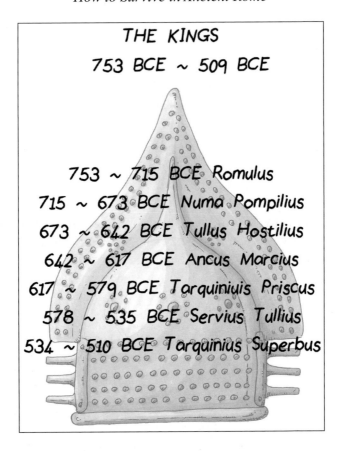

THE KINGS
753 BCE ~ 509 BCE

753 ~ 715 BCE Romulus
715 ~ 673 BCE Numa Pompilius
673 ~ 642 BCE Tullus Hostilius
642 ~ 617 BCE Ancus Marcius
617 ~ 579 BCE Tarquiniuis Priscus
578 ~ 535 BCE Servius Tullius
534 ~ 510 BCE Tarquinius Superbus

Rhea Silvia, to become a Vestal Virgin.[5] This well-thought-out plan was thwarted by the intervention of the god Mars – in that annoying way that gods[6] do – by impregnating Rhea Silvia with twin boys.

Furious, Amulius ordered that the twins (named Romulus and Remus) be drowned in the river Tiber. This would have been a very short book had they succeeded, but thankfully Amulius' henchmen turned out to be the lazy kind. Rather than throw the boys into the deepest part of the river, which would have involved effort and a decent overarm, they chucked them into a sluggish patch of water near the bank. The river receded and left the twins safely on dry land.

A passing she-wolf happened to stumble across the twins, and she suckled the hungry babies until they were rescued by a shepherd and his wife.[7] Royal twins Romulus and Remus grew up as humble shepherds; tending to their flocks, wandering about the picturesque landscape, and generally being no trouble to anyone.

> ## DID YOU KNOW?
>
> The hut where Romulus and Remus rested in-between flock tending is amazingly still standing 800 years later. It is on the Palatine Hill.[8]

This quiet life ended when the adult twins decided to attend a festival in a nearby town. Roman historian, Livy, describes this festival: 'Young men ran about naked and disposed themselves in various pranks and fooleries.'[9]

This sort of activity could only lead to trouble, and it did. Romulus did a runner, leaving Remus to be arrested and taken in chains to King Amulius. Back home the kindly shepherd decided this was the moment to reveal all to Romulus about his royal ancestry. This, along with the injustice of Remus' incarceration, inflamed Romulus. He and his gang of shepherds decided now was the time to overthrow the king.

It was a surprisingly quick and decisive victory and once Amulius was overthrown the twins decided they needed a city to rule, because that is what royalty does. Unlike Aeneas and the kings of Alba, the twins noticed that the nearby Palatine Hill was the perfect place on which to build a city. They set about sorting out all those niggly building regulations that possibly scuppered Aeneas' bid to found Rome.

One question lingered: which of them would be the king of this new city? There was only one way to decide: ask the gods. A suitable god response would have been 'why don't both of you rule as joint kings, you can have double thrones and a crown each,' but no, the gods instead sent vultures overhead to signify who they felt should be king. Remus saw six vultures, Romulus saw twelve, so the winner was Romulus.

Remus, in the manner of all thwarted brothers, had a bit of a sulk, then thought, 'screw him' and began to build his own city that he would rule completely by himself. This would be no fun unless Romulus knew all about it, so Remus wandered over to the Palatine Hill to tell his brother just how much better his city would be and how rubbish Romulus' walls were looking.

What the hapless Remus did not know was that Romulus suffered from a great sensitivity about his DIY. When Remus ill-advisedly jumped over his brother's newly built walls in a mocking manner, laughing about how crap they were, Romulus was enraged and beat him to death, which at least sorted out the succession neatly.

Romulus ruled as the sole king, doing all the things that kings usually do: fighting neighbouring towns, stealing their women and filling his new city with dispossessed criminals and bandits from other towns.[10] Then, just when he'd run out of neighbours to fight, he vanished. Literally. We are told that a mist descended and enveloped the king, and when it lifted Romulus was nowhere to be seen.

Roman historian, Livy, is open to the possibility that Romulus was torn to pieces by his own senators, and though it is true that it has the whiff of a story concocted in some haste and without much consideration given to the practical details (a literal smoke screen), we'd recommend you stick to the official line for your own safety as a visitor to the city.

After Romulus, Rome had six more kings, who set about formulating bits of Roman society that you will come to recognise, such as the religion, the law and the social classes. During the era of the kings Rome went from being a small brick wall handcrafted by Romulus to a town made up of many brick walls and which was beginning to annoy the neighbours by getting into fights with them.[11]

The monarchy, therefore, was trundling along nicely, founding stuff that proved useful later on and becoming the feisty, aggressive nation we all recognise. But then along came Rome's seventh and (*spoiler alert*) last king. He possessed a truly fabulous name: Tarquinius Superbus.

Superbus translates as arrogant, and Tarquinius was certainly that. Having seized the throne illegally, he decided to hold onto it by fear. He quickly earned the hatred of Romans by wrongful convictions, sudden executions, and most heinous of all, arranging a meeting at dawn then not turning up until sunset, thus giving ample time for the aggrieved parties to air their resentments.

When a snake crawled out of a wooden post in the palace, all foresaw it as a sign that Superbus was on the way out. The final push came when Superbus' son, Sextus, raped a married noblewoman by the name of Lucretia.

Most outraged by this outrage was Lucius Junius Brutus, who declared: 'By this girl's blood – none more chaste till a tyrant wronged her – and by the gods, I swear that with sword and fire, and whatever else I can lend my strength to my arm, I shall pursue Lucius Tarquinius the Proud, his wicked wife, and all his children, and never again will I let them or any other man be King in Rome.'[12]

It was a terrifically empowering speech, and more impressively, Brutus did exactly what he promised he would do. He got rid of Tarquinius

Superbus and his family, there were no more kings of Rome and Brutus was given the nickname 'The Liberator' as a result.

The Republic

Dates: 509 BCE–27 BCE (approximately)

THE REPUBLIC
509 BCE ~ 27 BCE

396~146 BCE Samnites, Greeks, Etruscans, Carthaginians and Italian allies conquered.

71 BCE Spartacus and his gladiator army conquered

67~62 BCE Pompey conquers the East

58~51 BCE   Julius Caesar conquers Gaul

49~48 BCE Caesar conquers Pompey in a civil war.

44 BCE Caesar assassinated

44~31 BCE Further civil wars

31 BCE Octavian conquers Antony and Cleopatra.

27 BCE Octavian renamed Augustus

Part One: The Rise

Having overthrown a tyrannical monarchy, the Romans were left with a governing gap; they filled it with a Republic. Under this system no one man could become too powerful and pull a Superbus. The top position of consul, for instance, was shared between two men for one year only, with restrictions on how soon they could become consul again. There was also a body of 600 men called the Senate. They had their own house built to contain them all while they debated and passed laws.

These senators and those laws were put to the people to vote on. Obviously by people we mean men and by men, we mean Roman men. Excluded entirely from the voting process were women, slaves and foreign residents of the city.

If we had to summarise the early Republican period in one word, that one word would be: wow. For this is the period when Rome grows from a small town to a fully blown, continent-stretching empire. This it did by near-constant warfare.

DID YOU KNOW?

The year 235 BCE is the only year during the Republican period where Roman was not at war with anyone.

During this period Rome battles against the Carthaginians in three separate wars, known collectively as the Punic Wars. Much in the manner of film sequels, the best of the Punic Wars was undoubtedly the second one, because it's the one with the elephants.[13]

Other wars were fought against the Samnites, the Etruscans, the Illyrians, the Macedonians, the Gauls, the Galatians, the Celts, the Achaeans, the Cimbri, the Numidians, the Sicilians, the Pontics, the Italian allies and the Syrians. As well as the odd internal fight.

With each victory more land was obtained, more riches stolen and more recruits for the army were enlisted. The latter was how Rome became so very successful, because they invited the male inhabitants of conquered territories to join their army, so they too could enjoy all the fun of conquest at somebody else's expense.[14]

Part Two: The (very) Bloody Fall

What goes up must come down, and so it was with the Roman Republic. After centuries of stampeding across Europe, North Africa and the East, the Republic faced its most deadly of enemies: itself.

In a terrible plot twist, the system of government that had led to all those crushing victories was the very reason the Roman Republic began to fall apart. From the mid-second century BCE onwards, Rome was engulfed in a series of brutal civil wars that ultimately destroyed the Republican system and led to a single man ruling all.

At the heart of this collapse was the inability of the Republican system to run a vast empire. Take the post of consul. Yes, it sounds great on papyri, two men sharing power only for one year. But if consul was the absolute highlight of your career, and would be referenced in the centuries to come, naturally you would want it to be spectacular, and well, memorable. You wouldn't want to spend it bogged down in boring and complicated problems like addressing the vast tracts of land that were finding themselves in the hands of the wealthy and thus dispossessing the poor. Who wants to be the consul whose year of power saw him start a bit of land reform?

And who says the next consul elected is going to want to be the one who continued a bit more land reform? Besides which, as consul, you are a member of the wealthy elite and have a very keen interest in land not being reformed (because you're making pots of money off your enormously huge farm situated on thousands of acres of land).

The Roman Republic was uniquely unable to deal with complicated issues that require continuity of thought and leadership. The offices of state began to strain under this pressure. Two factions formed as a result:

- The *Optimates* (or good men) who favoured sticking with Rome's ancient customs and beliefs. After all, it had served them bloody well so far. Why mess with success? Also lurking was a fear of what would happen if the ordinary Roman had more say in the system. This is not solely elitist snobbery: the ordinary Romans on the street had a mob form tendency that whirled through the city on a semi-regular basis.
- The *Populares*, who sided with the people of Rome and who recognised that wholesale reform was needed. They also recognised that they could win popular favour with a bit of coinage sprinkle,

and that having your own mob was not only super cool but kind of handy in helping you secure your position.

The clashes between these two schools of thought lead to a notable upturn in political skulduggery and murder, as each side sought to entrench their position in Rome. In 133 BCE, Tribune of the Plebs, Tiberius Gracchus sought to get his land reform bill passed by removing his fellow tribune, Octavius, from office. Such (illegal) antics terrified the good men of the senate, as did Gracchus' large popular support. In a worsening climate of fear and rumour, Gracchus and 300 of his supporters were beaten to death. Amongst the gang that attacked them were the noble senators who smashed wooden chairs to create makeshift weapons.

DID YOU KNOW?

One of Tiberius Gracchus' supporters was tracked down and executed in a particularly horrible fashion. He was shut in a large jar with snakes.

Gracchus' death was the start of mob violence as a way of securing political advantage. His younger brother, Gaius Gracchus, was decapitated in the Forum ten years later for trying to introduce much the same laws. Twenty years after Gaius Gracchus' death, Tribune of the Plebs, Saturninus secured the passing of his legislation by using his hired band of soldiers to menace the senate into passing it.

Not to be outdone another tribune, Sulpicius, surrounded himself with 600 equestrians[15] and used them to storm consular and public meetings. This worked out well for him because he narrowly escaped death by lynching by setting his mob on the attacking mob.

The violence became increasingly extreme and the political system was utterly unable to deal with it, with the result that a series of brutal civil wars kicked off. These, in the main, were led by Rome's increasingly charismatic generals who, unlike consuls, served in their provinces a great many years longer and could therefore build up a loyal base from their soldiers.[16] The ultimate victor of these was Julius Caesar. A *populares*, he took the title of dictator in perpetuity and set about reforming Rome. Unfortunately, he didn't get long to do his reforming[17] since he was assassinated on the Ides of March 44 BCE by another Brutus. This Brutus did less well on the inspiring speeches and was forced to flee Rome pretty damn quick.[18]

The Empire

Dates 27 BCE to present day

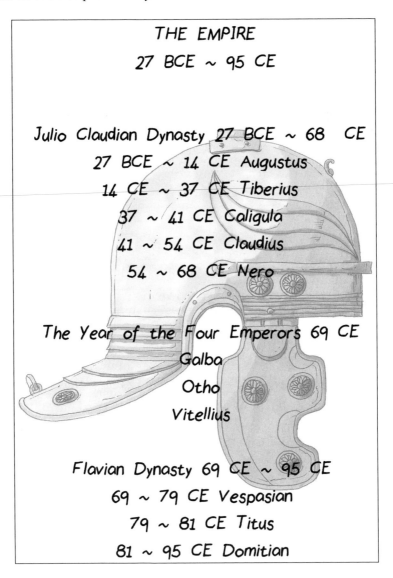

THE EMPIRE
27 BCE ~ 95 CE

Julio Claudian Dynasty 27 BCE ~ 68 CE
27 BCE ~ 14 CE Augustus
14 CE ~ 37 CE Tiberius
37 ~ 41 CE Caligula
41 ~ 54 CE Claudius
54 ~ 68 CE Nero

The Year of the Four Emperors 69 CE
Galba
Otho
Vitellius

Flavian Dynasty 69 CE ~ 95 CE
69 ~ 79 CE Vespasian
79 ~ 81 CE Titus
81 ~ 95 CE Domitian

Julius Caesar's murder did not result in the end of men seeking power by way of armed gangs/actual armies. Instead it started up another season of civil wars.

Firstly, Caesar's grieving pal, Mark Antony, teamed up with Caesar's great nephew, Octavian, to avenge themselves against foul assassinators, Brutus and Cassius, which they did at the Battle of Philippi, where Brutus and Cassius were both killed.

Mark Antony and Octavian carved up the empire between them; Antony took the east (including Egypt) and Octavian took the west. At first glance Antony seemed to have got the better deal. The east was way richer and more fun than the west, particularly a certain Egyptian queen named Cleopatra. However, Octavian held Italy, which meant that when he got annoyed with Antony he could rally the senators to declare him an enemy and vote for a war. Antony and Cleopatra perished, leaving Octavian, at the tender age of thirty-four,[19] sole master of Rome and her empire. To celebrate, Octavian changed his name to the far catchier Augustus and became Rome's first proper emperor.

The Emperors

Augustus 27 BCE–14 CE

Augustus successfully ended the civil wars that had plagued Rome for over a century. He was aided by the fact that everybody was sick of war – most of the elite families had been wiped out during the chaos – and that he was really very clever. We know this because he wrote a 4,000-word essay entitled *Res Gestae*, which can be summed up as: I am brilliant at everything. This was plastered up all over Rome and the empire, just in case anyone was unaware that Augustus was brilliant at everything. Rome's first proper emperor ushered in a period of peace and prosperity, which he handed over to his stepson, Tiberius.

Tiberius 14 CE–37 CE

One thing Augustus wasn't so brilliant at was securing an heir. Mostly this was due to his own longevity: four of his proposed heirs died before him, leaving only his stepson, Tiberius.

Stepfather and stepson had a rather strained relationship. This can be traced back to the time Augustus forced him to divorce the wife he loved and marry Augustus' daughter, Julia, who he did not like at all. When Tiberius followed his ex-wife around the market sobbing, Augustus took measures to ensure they never met again. This sort of thing tends to fester inside.

Tiberius was the brooding type, which was fully on display when he became emperor upon Augustus' death in 14 CE. Finding Rome too jolly for a proper sulk, he decamped to the island of Capri, leaving his Praetorian Prefect,[20] Sejanus, in charge. This proved a somewhat cataclysmic error as Sejanus took to bumping off the imperial family one by one. The result was that on Tiberius' death there was only one possible heir left standing: Caligula.

Caligula 37–41 CE

His name was actually Gaius. Caligula was a nickname roughly meaning 'bootykins' after the replica military boots he wore as a toddler. Caligula did not have a great childhood. His father, Germanicus, died when he was only seven. His mother and two brothers fell to Sejanus' dastardly scheme. Caligula himself only narrowly escaped Sejanus' shiny death warrant signing pen.

It's hardly surprising that Emperor Caligula was somewhat troubled, to put it mildly. To put it more strongly, he was sadistically unhinged to such a degree that there seemed no other option than horribly hack him to death.[21] Or perhaps they feared that Caligula's boast that his horse would make a better senator would prove accurate. Nobody likes to be outshone by Dobbinus.

Claudius 41–54 CE

The assassination of Caligula left the emperor's personal bodyguard with a dilemma. No emperor equals no emperor's bodyguard. Fearing unemployment, they set off to find a new emperor to (badly) guard and found Caligula's uncle, Claudius, hiding behind a curtain. Deciding he was good enough, they carried him up to the palace as the new emperor.

The palace guard were mostly right; Claudius was good enough. Though he was let down by his licentious nature, which saw him change the law so he could marry his niece, Agrippina. This backfired on him spectacularly when Agrippina poisoned[22] him so that her son, Nero, would succeed

Nero 54–68 CE

Nero was a victim of Rome's misogyny. A seventeen-year-old youth when he became emperor, he wanted nothing more than to watch chariot races, write poetry and fool about with the palace slaves. However, his mother, Agrippina, was politics mad. Excluded from all governmental positions due to her being a woman, she was forced to satisfy her political urges vicariously through her son.

DID YOU KNOW?

Nero was officially married three times, but also had two unofficial marriages: as the bride to his ex-slave, Pythagorus, and as the groom to the eunuch, Sporus.

It worked for a while, until Nero got fed up with mother knowing best (because he knew she did) and had her killed. Which is about as low as you can go. Unless of course you're Nero and you still have nine years to reign. There were many victims of Nero, from Christians to senators to his own family. But a special mention goes to the hundreds of people who suffered greatly and for many hours during Nero's poetry recitals.[23]

Eventually the ruling classes decided they could not bear any more iambic pentameters and made the non-poet Galba emperor instead. Nero fled Rome and committed suicide aged thirty.

The Year of the Four Emperors 69 CE
After Nero's death we see a return of the type of bloody chaos that afflicted the late Republic. However, the empire is much more efficiently run than the Republic, and so the bloody chaos only lasts a year. A year in which Galba, Otho and Vitellius all come and go (horribly) leaving one man standing, Titus Flavius Vespasian.

Vespasian 69–79 CE
Vespasian does an Augustus and restores peace and prosperity to Rome after the brutal and bloody year of the four emperors. He does this without feeling the need to boast about it in 4,000 words and plaster it all over the city. After ten years of calm ruling, Vespasian suffers a bit of 'tummy trouble' [24] and dies.

Titus 79–81 CE
Titus, the eldest son of Vespasian, was a hero of the Jewish wars.[25] Although Titus only ruled for two years, he packed in a fair amount of

disasters in that time, including plague, fire and that volcano that's really famous for blowing its top all over Pompeii.[26] He completed this list of catastrophes by unexpectedly dying of a fever before he'd had a chance to do anything properly emperor-like.

Domitian 81 CE to present day

Domitian is the younger son of Vespasian. He has ruled for fourteen years. He's marvellous in every way.[27]

Having taken a quick tour through 800 years of history, it is now time for you to explore your destination. But before you hit the streets of first-century Rome we have some basic information that will make your visit go all the smoother.

What is Rome like in 95 CE?

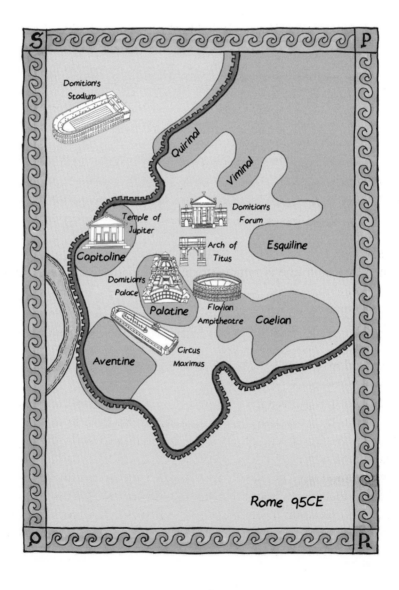

It's large. Very large. A century ago Emperor Augustus was boasting that he gifted money to 300,000 Romans. By Romans we mean male citizens so double that figure to include women. Throw children, slaves and foreign-born non-citizens into the pot, give it a stir, let it steam for a bit and we've likely got a population bubbling at a million people, spread over its seven hills. To put this in some kind of context, it took until 1801 for London to have a similar sized population.

Rome is very, very busy, and very, very noisy. There have been some attempts to deal with these issues. The law states that goods may not be transported into the city during daylight, which is very sensible. Who wants to compete for space with a rolling wagon full of amphora or slaves, let alone animal stock being herded to the markets? How would anyone go about their business? Or avoid getting their sandaled foot painfully run over?

Unimpeded pavements are a bonus and you may walk about the city in a much freer manner. However, the downside of the wagon law is that all goods are therefore transported overnight: when all of Rome is trying to get to sleep. As the local writer, Juvenal says jadedly: 'Insomnia causes most deaths here.'[28]

Rome is spread across seven (famous) hills, they are: Quirinal, Viminal, Esquiline, Caelian, Aventine, Palatine and Capitoline. The Palatine, you will remember, is where Romulus laid down the very first bricks of the city. Nowadays it is home to the sprawling imperial palace. The nearby Capitoline is famous for its humungous Temple of Jupiter, which has an unfortunate habit of burning down.[29]

The Esquiline is where you will find some very pleasant public gardens. We highly recommend the gardens of Maecenas. It is also home to some truly awful bars in the dodgy Subura district, which we highly recommend avoiding. Unless you are a connoisseur of dodgy bars, in which case you are in for a treat!

The Quirinal is famous for being the hill on which our current emperor was born and raised. To commemorate this glorious moment in history, a temple has been built to the Flavian family on the very spot of his childhood home.

The Aventine is where you will find the docks and muscled dock workers (if that's your fancy). There are some luxurious mansions owned by Rome's super rich to be found on the Caelian Hill, and the Viminal Hill is the location of the Praetorian Barracks, which are to be avoided at all costs!

As you may have gathered, Rome is quite hilly. Bring comfortable footwear.

Time

i) Years and Months

Though we have spoken of this as the year 95 CE, the Romans do not know it as such. They count their years from the foundation of Rome in 753 BCE, therefore the year is 848. Most Romans, however, refer to the year by the names of the consuls serving: 95 CE is the Consulship of Titus Flavius Clemens and Domitian Caesar.[30]

The Ancient Greeks had an alternative way of dating the years; they used the Olympic Games. For example, the Persian invasion of Greece in 480 BCE is said to have occurred in the year of the seventy-fifth Olympiad. There has been an attempt to duplicate this by the Romans in the shape of the Secular Games. Revived by Augustus in 17 BCE, these were to be held every 110 years. But the next set of Secular Games were held by Claudius a mere thirty years later, mucking up the calculations entirely. In recent years though Emperor Domitian has restaged the Secular Games, and at the proper interval from Augustus' original set.

In a similar vein, Nero installed an arts festival, the Neronia, to be held every five years. Only, like Claudius, he got too excited and couldn't wait five whole years for the next one. With similar impatience, while touring Greece, Nero couldn't wait for the next Olympic Games to be held so he forced the Greeks to reschedule them, thus completely buggering up their calendar as well.

There are twelve months in a year, and all will be familiar to you, except for September and October. The emperor has recently renamed these months Germanicus and Domitianus after himself. Which is the sort of thing all of us would do if granted unlimited power.[31]

ii) Days

Roman months are split into the:

> Kalends – first day of the month.
> Nones – fifth or seventh day of the month.
> Ides – thirteenth or fifteenth day of the month.

All dates are calculated from these. Such as:

> 'God Jupiter above! Guess what? It's only two before the
> Ides of March! That's come around quickly again.'
> Or
> 'God Jupiter above! Guess what? It's only the Ides of March
> today.'
> Or
> 'God Jupiter above! Guess what? It's two after the Ides of
> March, it seems months ago now.'

Another thing to be aware of is that certain days are marked as unlucky. During these days, known as *nefasti*, it's best to avoid undertaking any new business deals (because you will get ripped off), any sort of building project (because a beam will likely fall on your head) and we certainly wouldn't advise trying out that new recipe you've been dying to at a very important dinner party you're holding (food poisoning all round at a minimum).

The best thing to do on a *nefastus* day is as little as possible. Perhaps laying on a couch in a darkened room carefully eating grapes. Though given that there are approximately 109 *nefasti* days in a year you might want to mix it up a bit to prevent tedium. If you're terrified of accidentally doing something important on a *nefastus* day don't panic, calendars are posted up outside most temples so you can check daily whether the gods are onside or not.

Temple calendars will also alert you to any festivals or feast days coming up. Which gives you ample time to get your poshest toga/gown laundered in preparation.

iii) Hours

The Roman day has twelve hours of daytime and twelve hours of night-time. So far so familiar, but the newcomer needs to be warned that these twelve hours are counted from sunrise to sunset. In winter the time between sunrise and sunset is shorter and in summer considerably longer. To ensure there is a standard twelve hours no matter what the time of year, the Romans simply change the length of the hour. In summer, therefore, a Roman hour can be up to thirty minutes longer than in the winter.

Yes, it is rather confusing, but don't worry because there are plenty of timekeeping devices available to help you keep track of time. Sundials are popular and you can even get portable ones for when you're on the move. Or you could invest in a water clock that measures the time via the dripping of liquid into a specially measured vessel.

If machinery isn't your thing then why not invest in a slave to count the hours for you, or else take Pliny the Elder's advice and purchase a cock 'which Nature designed for interrupting sleep and waking men to work.' Though you might want to check in with the neighbours before investing in bird ownership. Nobody wants to find their alarm clock dumped on their doorstep with its neck wrung.

Alternatively, you could live it like a local and pay no attention to the time at all. Unless you are fighting a court case, when you will need to be at a particular place at a particular time, the hours won't have much meaning to you.

Rome's relaxed attitude to time is reflected in the tale of its first ever sundial. It was a gift from Sicily and was installed proudly in the Forum in 263 BCE. Ninety-nine years later some clever wag discovered it was wrongly calibrated and had been telling the wrong time for nearly a century. That nobody noticed, or even cared, in all that time shows how little Romans care about keeping time.

Money

Money comes in coins and is split into four standard denominations: *As*, *sestertius*, *denarius* and the *aureus*. The *sestertius* is a brass coin worth four *asses*. The *denarius* is a silver coin which is worth four *sestertius*. The *aureus* is a gold coin worth around twenty-five *denarii*.

To give you some insight into monetary values, and therefore protect you from those that would take advantage of a newcomer to Rome: you should only pay around five *denarii* for twenty loaves worth of grain, a couple of *assess* for hay to feed your horse, 400 *denarii* for a decent pair of carrier pigeons, 1000 *sesterces* for a quarter of a hector of farmland and fifty million *sesterces* for a particularly fine eunuch boy.[32]

We'd recommend rounding up any feral pigeons to fool the neighbours into thinking that you have more money than you do. Or perhaps a favourite nephew would like to put it about he's been 'done'. Appearances are everything in Rome.

Transport

As noted above, wagons are forbidden within the city walls during daytime hours, so alternative transport will need to be found to travel about. Thankfully Rome is easily walkable, though overcrowding can make progress slow on the pavements and who knows what you might step in. To this end you might want to hire or purchase a litter.

A litter is a couch held on four poles that are carried by bearers. Litters are perfect for those who want to travel about the city without spoiling their footwear, or who are the busy sort who can't waste valuable working time. The size of a litter can easily accommodate both you and your transcribing slave, and you can recline on soft cushions while getting on with that all-important paperwork. Though do remember to draw back the curtains if you want everyone to see how busy and important you are. A thoughtful pose with stylus pressed against your forehead, we find, works wonders with your reputation as an intellectual.

Similarly, if you have purchased a particularly nifty looking litter you will obviously want those curtains open to show off that it is yours.

Names

Roman names can seem quite bewildering to the outsider. People may have one name (women and slaves), two names, three names or an entire sentence of names (looking at you Gaius Julius Caesar Octavianus Divi Filius[33]).

This can all be a bit confusing, particularly when trying to work out by which name to address someone. Slaves are the easiest to practise on; if you are unsure of their name, simply address them as 'boy' or 'girl'. This holds true even if the slave has white hair, three teeth and wrinkles you could hide a grape in. You might want to dress it up with a 'you boy' and a casually delivered insult on their appearance to distinguish them from any other slaves present.

Men

The most common name combination for men is the three-namer.

The first of these is known as the *praenomen* and is a personal name used by those closest to them. There's not a great variety of these; only eighteen regularly feature and amongst the most common are Gaius, Marcus, Lucius, Publius, Aulus, Titus and Tiberius. This is something to remember when visiting the local bars, for example. It is highly unlikely there will only be one Marcus present at any given time. Yelling out, 'Marcus, it's your round, you tight ****' is sure to lead to all kinds of trouble. The *praenomen*, therefore, is best used within a small household. Though as most sons are named after their fathers this only works in households of one.

The second name, *the nomen*, denotes the family or gens. Sort of like a surname, it's the Julius in Gaius Julius Caesar and will be applied to every male in the family.

So far, so not very useful in distinguishing individuals. Which is why Roman men have a third name, the *cognomen*. *Cognomens* are often a nickname based on appearance, such as Rufus, meaning red, which is liberally applied to those with ginger hair. Or if you are feeling particularly ill disposed towards your offspring, Verrucosus, which means warty.[34] See also Cicero, meaning chickpea, the result of an unfortunate nose addition of an ancestor to the famous Cicero.[35]

Other *cognomens* might be awarded for amazing acts. Plain old Gaius Pompey became Gaius Pompey Magnus (the Great) because of his successful campaigning in the East. Publius Cornelius Scipio acquired Africanus as a *cognomen* after successfully beating Hannibal.

To demonstrate the impossible nature of Roman names, let us look at the emperor's own family:

> His grandfather – Titus Flavius Sabinus
> His father – Titus Flavius Vespasian
> His uncle – Titus Flavius Sabinus
> His brother – Titus Flavius Vespasian
> His cousins – Titus Flavius Sabinus and Titus Flavius Clemens
> His name – Titus Flavius Domitian

That's a lot of Titus Flaviuses. Also note the naming of sons with the exact same name as their fathers. It's hardly surprising that, as emperor,

Domitian couldn't wait to add extra names to his own in order to distance himself from all those other Titus Flaviuses. His imperial name is Titus Flavius Caesar Domitian Augustus Germanicus. The Caesar and Augustus are acquired to denote his role as emperor; the Germanicus to commemorate his victories in Germany. Should you, by some freak chance get to meet the emperor, make sure you use all of his names to address him.

Women

It's even worse for women, so brace yourself. Women have one or perhaps two names. They are named after their father. Julius Caesar had a daughter named Julia. Mark Antony had a daughter named Antonia. Augustus' right-hand man, Agrippa, named his daughter Agrippina. In keeping with this theme, our friend Hortensia was named after her father, Hortensius.

Whereas with men you might alter the *cognomen* when you get to the second son and so forth, with women nobody seems to care about distinguishing them. The Emperor Augustus had two sisters, both called Octavia. Mark Antony's two daughters were called Antonia and yes, you've guessed it, Antonia. To distinguish between Antonias or, indeed, Julias, you will find Major and Minors dished out to the elder and younger daughters. If you have more than two daughters, that's your own fault and we can help you no further.

Slave names

Slaves have only one name, which is chosen by their master. Greek names are popular for slaves, such as our friend Ajax who shares a name with a hero of Greek mythology. Elsewhere you might find a Narcissus or a Pallas.[36] The most popular name for male slaves is Felix, meaning happy or lucky. Which given their status is somewhat of a cruel jibe.

You do occasionally stumble across slaves with the unfortunate name of Erotica or Eroticus. Similarly, Nero named a favourite slave Sporus, which means 'seed' and was a nasty joke on the poor lad, since as a eunuch he did not possess any.

On being freed, a slave will take their master's or mistress's name to add to their own. Our friend, Titus Flavius Ajax, owns the first two names of the emperor, his former master. Male slaves freed under emperors Claudius, Nero and Tiberius have the first two names of Tiberius

Claudius. Female imperial slaves will take the singular female name of their mistress to add to their own. This adds to household confusion significantly, since not only do you have members of the family sharing the same name but also any freed slaves in the house.

Language

The official language in Rome is Latin, though most of the elite class will also be fluent in Greek. There is a high level of literacy amongst all classes in ancient Rome. This is evident from the really quite filthy graffiti that you can expect to find on pretty much any spare piece of wall.

Chapter 1

Social Structure

Social class in Rome involves all kinds of questions, such as, are you:

- Patrician or plebeian?
- Senatorial or equestrian?
- Free or freed?
- Citizen or non-citizen?
- Italian or provincial?
- Are you a member of the infamia?

Your answer to the above questions will determine much about your life. Including whether you pay tax, who you can marry, what public positions you can hold and what clothes you can wear.

We are here to guide you through the complex world of Roman social class and save you any embarrassments incurred by accidentally breaking social conventions. It's also nice to know your place and associated rights, should you ever find yourself in trouble. We really don't want you being thrown to the beasts in the arena, do we?

What is the social structure in ancient Rome?

At the top is the emperor, followed by those of senatorial rank, then those of equestrian ranks, ordinary Roman citizens without rank, freedman (ex-slaves) and at the bottom slaves and women.

This structure is visually represented in public spaces like the amphitheatre[1] where the seating arrangements have women and slaves at the very top and senators with a good blood-splatter view right by the arena side.

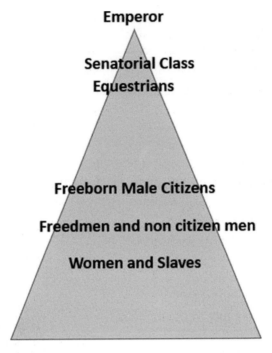

The Social Classes.

Other ways to spot someone's rank is by the purple stripes on their toga. Senators have a broad purple stripe, equestrians a narrow purple stripe, and everyone else doesn't bother with togas at all unless it is an unseasonably special occasion.

At the lower end of the social scale freedmen are permitted to wear a liberty cap, also known as a Phrygian hat, to denote their freed status. Though one does wonder how often this is checked and what barriers there are in place to stop a slave knitting his own liberty cap and using it to avoid rough treatment while out doing business for his master.

Slaves are generally indistinguishable from the free population in their attire, though some wealthier households like to dress their staff in matching coloured tunics to show off that they own a large number of slaves.

Senatorial Rank

If you want to hold the highest public office, on the career ladder the Romans call the *cursus honorum*,[2] you will need to hold senatorial rank.

The good news is that the senatorial class is not a closed shop. Many men have entered the senate as the first in their family to do so. Compared to the old Roman Republic, the Roman Empire is much more open to new men, chiefly because the old families mostly got wiped out in the civil wars that preceded Augustus. You don't have to be Roman, or even Italian to, qualify: the Emperor Claudius opened the senate to the Gauls, which admittedly did not go down too well with traditionalists.[3]

That's the good news. The bad news is that to qualify as a senator does not come cheap. You will need cash and land holdings worth at least one million sesterces. Oh, and you can't have obtained that fortune in trade. Senators are not allowed to grubby their hands in the murky world of trade.

A million sesterces is a lot of money. It really is. To put it in some context, Roman legionaries earn around 1200 sesterces per year and are considered well paid.

There are, of course, benefits to being a senator. You get that great seat at the Games. You get that purple broad stripe on your toga. If you make it to being a provincial governor, you get a whole province of people to rip off and help you enrich yourself. You also have the chance to be close to the emperor. Closeness to the emperor is a key way to keep that million sesterces topped up, for influence is a commodity brought and sold in Rome.

Conversely, the negatives of being a senator also include closeness to the emperor. The closer you are to the emperor the more likely you are to irritate him in some way that he can only see being resolved by you being dead.

The Senate House.

DID YOU KNOW?

Augustus and Mark Antony decided to wipe out their political enemies and improve their finances by executing 2,000 notable citizens and stealing their property.

Equestrians

In the depths of history, it is generally supposed that the equestrians must have had something to do with horses, hence the name. But nobody knows what. These days they have little to do with stables, but rather serve as the class between senators and everyone else.

The senators see it as their birth right to serve in all the top positions in Rome and assist the emperor in ruling the empire properly. However, several generations of emperors have discovered that having a million sesterces and a good name does not automatically make you any good at administrating and ruling.

Also the senatorial class have twigged that whole being close to the emperor/execution link, and have thus ducked out of public service in order to preserve for longer the attachment of their head to their neck.[4] To this end there are the equestrians, who fill those position the senators won't, or can't, do for the emperor. This can be a source of resentment for the senators, but really what can they do about it except moan while sitting on top of a pile of million sesterces?

DID YOU KNOW?

The Censor could expel senators from the senate for dubious morals. One senator was kicked out for daring to kiss his wife in public during daylight hours.

To qualify for the equestrian rank you need 300,000 sesterces, which is still a lot of money, and you don't even get a horse for that! But the equestrian rank is, unlike the senatorial class, open to ex-slaves, and it's a handy way for the emperor to fill public position with people he knows to be capable.

The upside to being an equestrian is, again, great seats at the Games, prestige, a purple stripe on the toga and closeness to the emperor. The downside is, again, closeness to the emperor. Equestrians are executed as often as senators, but historians don't generally bother to name them. This means they miss out on that whole 'making an honourable stand' legacy.

How rich is rich?

There is a certain image that's been passed down of ancient Rome as a city corrupted by wealth and decadence on an epic scale; one which is not without foundation. Though a million sesterces is the minimum qualifying wealth for senatorial rank, there are people whose wealth far exceeded this and who spend vast sums on some really quite ridiculous things.

- An unnamed soul spent 30,000 sesterces on three mullets, a purchase so outrageous that the Emperor Tiberius suggested laws limiting what could be charged for certain items.[5]
- A lady named Gegania spent 50,000 sesterces on candelabra.
- Calvisius Sabinus spent 100,000 sesterces on a slave that could quote the entirety of Homer from memory. He also trained up other slaves to similarly memorise Hesiod and other poets.
- Nightingales were more expensive to purchase than many slaves. There is a story that one Roman paid 600,000 sesterces for a single white nightingale; money that could buy you the service of 500 soldiers for a year to spend locating white nightingales and commandeering them on your behalf.
- Gaius Caecilius Isidorus, a former slave, spent over a million sesterces on his funeral.
- The Emperor Vitellius spent a million sesterces on a single earthenware dish (we have to assume it was a big one).

DID YOU KNOW?

Politician Marcus Licinius Crassus maintained you could only call yourself rich if you could support a legion of soldiers on your yearly income.

Freedmen

Though they're lumped altogether as one single rank, there is much variety and strata of ex-slaves. Former imperial slaves in charge of palace departments, for instance, are unlikely to have much in common with a freed farm worker who spent his days raking muck. Though, come to think of it, there might be some similarity there after all.

Rome is unique in ancient slave-owning societies in the scale of how many slaves could buy their freedom, for many Romans slavery was a temporary status. But clearly one they preferred not to recall, for Roman literature is almost entirely devoid of slave or ex-slave voices.[6]

The huge numbers of slaves freed has created quite a large class of freedmen. They are barred from certain public offices, cannot serve in the army and are forbidden to marry women of equestrian or senatorial status. This doesn't mean there are no relationships between the elite and the freed. Emperor Vespasian's long-term mistress was the ex-Imperial slave, Antonia Caenis. Although officially they could not marry, he very much treated her as his wife. However, freedmen could become citizens, run businesses and acquire equestrian rank.

DID YOU KNOW?

Emperor Nero wanted desperately to marry ex-slave Acte and bribed two senators to say she was nobly born to make the marriage legal. They didn't marry.[7]

The freedmen we hear about most, and usually in a negative way, are the imperial freedman. These were the freed slaves of the emperor. Accounts of imperial freedmen reek of jealousy and snobbery. There is a general disgust that ex-slaves have risen to such positions of power and obtained such wealth that is surely the right of the senatorial class.

It is most unfair too. His Imperial Majesty, Domitian, is keen to promote those who have actual ability, as opposed to a nice name. Is it our fault that we imperial freedmen possess talent? It would be a crime not to use our superior faculties to aid the emperor at all times.

The problem with senators is that they haven't twigged that their tendency to plot against emperors and be too demanding about what they are entitled to, might make them a bit annoying. On the other hand, that capable slave in the petitions office who always treats you like the best thing ever in a purple cloak and garland is far more palatable.

Titus Flavius Ajax

As Ajax has neglected to mention it, we should point out that imperial freedmen are not above plotting the assassination of the emperor. They just tend to be far better at it than their senatorial counterparts.[8]

Slaves and Women

Women are officially classed beneath freedmen due to a distinct lack of rights. In law, both slaves and women are in the custodianship of another and have no autonomy to make their own decisions. In the case of women, there's a big question over how much of this is actually practised, but slaves certainly have no will of their own and are entirely at the mercy of their master. This is not at all pleasant, though, as we've seen, slaves have a good chance of ceasing to be slaves via manumission.

Unfortunately, women have no such route to an improved situation. Or do they? Pliny the elder assures us, 'That women have changed into men is not a myth.'[9] One such transformation Pliny claims to have witnessed himself. So there is, apparently, always a chance that ancient Roman women can escape their limited rights by way of a gender transmogrification. We'd recommend not investing too much hope in that eventuality.

DID YOU KNOW?

Freedman Gaius Caecilius Isidorus owned 4,116 slaves. In his possession were also 257,000 cows and 60 million sesterces in cash.

Infamia

Beneath even slaves in the social pecking order are the *infamia*. Which is odd because amongst this class are some of the most famous people in Rome. The *infamia* are made up of those participating in taboo/dubious occupations: these include prostitution, dancing, acting and being a gladiator.

You could also enter the ranks of the *infamia* by certain socially unacceptable behaviours. *Infamia* is the ultimate in social shaming and they are non-citizens with few legal rights. All of which means that the rest of Rome can look down on them with a superior smugness, which is really what we all want from life.

However, there are those who are drawn to the whiff of a taboo; who dare to risk a dalliance on the edges of society, who seek to scandalise society by *cough* overfamiliarity with the *infamia*. Women have been known to go wild for a bit of gladiator fraternisation. Men have been known to floozy themselves all over actresses. Even the empress has involved herself with a bit of infamy with a member of the *infamia*; the actor, Paris.

We cannot stress strongly enough the wisdom of never, ever, ever mentioning the Empress Domitia's behaviour out loud, or written down or, actually, best not even to think of it in your head. Although the emperor welcomed the empress back after her affair and resulting exile, he is still a little touchy about it; as demonstrated by the recent execution of a man for the crime of looking a bit like Paris.

What else do I need to know about Roman social classes?

You may hear the terms patrician or plebeian bandied about. If you're wondering how you know which you are, it is very simple. If you have to ask, then you are definitely a pleb.

Nobody really knows what the original distinction was, but patricians seem to have coveted and held onto key ruling positions from almost the birth of Rome. They maintain that this is because they are clever men ideally suited to ruling and should thus be left to get on with it.

There have been some flash points in the past when the plebs have disputed this and grabbed a bit more for themselves. They have their own public official in the shape of the Tribune for the Plebs, a position that in Republican days had a higher than average brutal murder rate. Today it's much less controversial.

DID YOU KNOW?

The extremely posh, patrician-born Publius Clodius changed his status by being adopted into a plebeian family. This allowed him to become the Tribune of the Plebs.[10]

Most of the old patrician families have died out, therefore the senatorial class these days is more pleb than patrician. The father of the current emperor, Domitian, was a pleb. The benefits of being a patrician, therefore, amount to bragging rights alone.

What's the difference between a citizen and a non-citizen?

What a question! You may as well ask what the difference is between a citizen and a plank of wood. A Roman citizen enjoys all the joys and rights of civilisation. A plank of wood does not.

Being a citizen confers you with a natural allure of honour and superiority. It also bestows you with a protective hide against being flogged, crucified or tortured. In today's world this is worth having. You are also entitled to appeal to the emperor. There's no guarantee he'll bother to open that appeal, but it's a nice to have a threat to bandy about.

DID YOU KNOW?

Citizenship status did not always save you from the worst. During the civil wars of 69 CE an aide to Galba, Icelus, was crucified despite his freedmen status.

Are there any conflicts between Roman social classes? Do those at the bottom ever rebel?

Not as much as you'd think given the vast differences between them. Though every decent Roman shudders at the name Spartacus.[11]

The lower classes often express their displeasure at the policies of their governing class by having a good old riot. As long as it lacks professional organisation this is to be shrugged off as normal political discourse.

9

What stops conflict between the classes is a social oil called *amicitia*. It translates as 'friendship', but that's not quite right. A more accurate translation would be 'you scratch my back and I'll scratch yours'. It's a dizzying swirl of favours that are offered and paid back. At the heart of this is the patron/client relationship.

A patron is someone of higher social standing with whom the client aligns themselves in the hope of benefiting from the friendship. Likewise, the patron hopes to benefit from the client in some way.

Obviously, the higher up the social strata the more desirable a man as a patron, which means you may have plenty of competition. It is not unknown for a patron to have hundreds of clients, particularly if he has a large number of slaves, as any freed slave is automatically the client of their former master. A freedman is expected to offer up whatever services his former master requires.[12] Freedom, therefore, doesn't always mean freedom.

In the case of our friend, Ajax, his patron is the emperor who freed him. But as emperors have thousands of freedmen from the palace staff, Ajax's experience of the patron/client relationship is likely to be looser than many. Though as an ex-slave of an emperor his imperial connections make him enticing as a patron.

What are the duties of a client?

To do whatever his patron wishes. The first hour of the day is when a client will visit his patron to see what help he may be. Be prepared to queue in an orderly fashion should your patron be a popular one. The patron himself will be seated in his atrium ready to receive all his clients, after which, if the patron has public business, his entire clientele accompanies him on his walk to the Senate House or law courts. Such a walk allows him to show off just how popular and influential he is to all. Also, it lowers his chances of being mugged.

How does a client benefit?

Hopefully, a client will benefit by having gained something of importance via his patron's influence. Or more likely than not, a place at his patron's dinner table where he will learn where he stands in the rungs of clients by the type and quantity of food he is served. After which he may well weigh up that such a meagre feast is not worth his efforts in getting up early.

Amicitia

As a very important imperial freedman,[13] I am frequently approached by individuals wishing me to use my influence with the emperor. I can fast-track your petition over all those other petty requests. I can pass your terrible poetry onto the emperor for his bedtime reading. I can subtly suggest to his Imperial Majesty that you'd be fantastic at whatever position it is that you want me to secure for you.

As I get so many of these requests I have worked out a system of prioritisation: what's in it for me?

This doesn't necessarily involve money (though it is always welcome), but more often than not it is a case of 'who do you know that I might like to know because knowing them might be useful to me in the future?' If I grant you a favour this might be a useful bargaining point when, ten years hence, I want to buy a plot of land that your aunt's husband is selling. I may well suggest you write to your uncle-in-law recommending me as a buyer and listing all the many favours I have granted you to prove my worth as a Roman citizen.

Likewise, should my grandson have his eyes on a public career, I can rely on you to put forward his name to your connections as a very suitable young man to serve as a military tribune.[14]

Chapter 2

Family

The Romans are big on family, both past and present: ancestors being just as important as descendants. The wealthy fill the atriums in their ample villas with the death masks of their deceased relatives, to impress upon the visitor how impressive a stock they come from. There are even festivals such as Parentalia, held in February each year, dedicated to honouring your ancestors.

DID YOU KNOW?

Julius Caesar went one step further with his boasts about his relatives. He claimed to be descended from the goddess Venus.

The Roman writer, Suetonius, dedicates the opening paragraphs of his emperor biographies with a thorough discussion of each imperial master's family history. A standard tactic in political manoeuvring is to smear your opponent's ancestry. Mark Antony, for instance, taunted the young Augustus with claims that his great-grandfather was a ropemaker.

Family is considered so important to the current emperor that he has instigated a series of morality laws dedicated to its preservation. These can be summed up as:

Marriage = good.
Lots of children = good.

Anything besides being married and having lots of children = bad, and all that is wrong about Rome these days.

DID YOU KNOW?

Penalties for being single start at age twenty for women and age twenty-five for men. Some men have escaped penalisation by marrying pre-pubescent girls.

Romans are of the strong belief that there was a golden age when men and women were morally perfect and untainted by any outside depravity. It was this moral character that led them to the fabulous conquests of the Republican era and the creation of their empire. The fact that they still have an empire, and a much bigger one at that, in these morally reprehensible times has in no way dented this obsession with the olden days.

We recommend you play along by periodically decrying divorce rates and expressing your desire to own a small farm in the countryside, where you will live an upright life by toiling in back-breaking work.

What does a Roman family look like, and how is it different to modern families?

There is a father, mother, children, extended family and, of course, any slaves the household own. One of the key differences about Roman families is the legal powers granted to the head of the household, known as the *pater familias*. This man, and it is always a man, is responsible for the household wealth and property.

What kind of powers does the *pater familias* have?

He has all the power. He is all powerful over all members of his household, even when they are adults. He has sole control of the finances of the entire household, even adult children. He chooses marriage partners for his children and can dissolve those marriages, should his in-laws be particularly irritating.

He can dish out whatever punishment he sees fit to any member of his household. Technically the *pater familias* could even murder family members if they failed to live up to his standards.[1]

DID YOU KNOW?

Egnatius Maetennus clubbed his wife to death for drinking wine. Another woman was starved to death by her family for stealing the keys to the wine cellar.

On the less brutal side, the *pater familias* has an important role maintaining the household shrine and keeping the household gods, the Lares, happy.

This all sounds like terrific fun. Who wouldn't like to wield the metaphorical and actual axe over all? Talk about power, as well as all that money you control!

But dig a little deeper and being the *pater familias* starts to sound a lot less fun. Yes, you can legally and morally give your disappointing adult son a good thrashing, but will he then bow to the all mighty *pater familias*? Some examples we have would suggest not.

Marcus Salvius Otho, briefly emperor in 69 CE, was so wild in his youth that his father was moved to flog him, a good Roman punishment to correct errant behaviour and firmly place a young man on the correct path to being a responsible adult. But it had absolutely no effect at all, for Otho continued his wild behaviour unabated and then upped the ante by infiltrating Nero's even wilder set.[2]

Or there's the father of Curio, who tried to stop his son's friendship with the malign influence of Mark Antony. Strong talks with his son did not work. Kicking Antony out of the house did not work. Putting guards on the door to stop Antony seeing his son did not work. Curio's father, we are told, sat on the bed and wept. Hardly the behaviour of an all-powerful patriarch.

Being stuck with the responsibility of adult sons can be more of a burden than a blessing. In the elite families the first public position is held around the age of twenty-five, this means there are an awful lot of posh boys from rich families with far too much time on their hands.

DID YOU KNOW?

The Emperor Vespasian's mother motivated him to start his public career by constant sarcasm, comparing him to his more driven older brother.

The young Caligula, for instance, was said to enjoy donning a robe and wig and hitting the town. Otho's floggable youthful pursuits involved wandering about the city bundling drunks and women into blankets and tossing them into the river Tiber. Mark Antony, so Cicero alleges, dressed as a woman and took up prostitution in his youth.

There are less alarming leisure activities available. Watching chariot racing, for instance. Or wrestling. Or the Games. Or placing high-stakes bets on all of them, a pastime that is all the more appealing when you have a living *pater familias* responsible for all the family finances: including debts.

Probably the best example of the struggling *pater familias* is the Emperor Augustus. Augustus made a big show of family. His series of morality laws included inducements to have three children or more, penalties for failing to marry and stiff punishment for adulterers.

He paraded his own family as an example to follow, sharing the strict education of his daughter, Julia, as the model.[3] He chose all three of Julia's husbands for her and arranged the marriages. The first was to her cousin, Marcellus. The second was to her father's right-hand man, Agrippa, who was over twenty years her senior. Her third marriage was to her stepbrother, Tiberius.

Augustus similarly orchestrated his male relatives' lives, appointing them to public positions from a young age and insisting that they serve the state in unending duty. This was how family was done properly, he declared to the world. This is the traditional *pater familias* role.

Naturally, it all went wrong. Daughter Julia, knee deep in woven underpants, embarked on a full-scale rebellion against her father. She did this by 'having some fun', saying 'things which might be considered by some stick in the mud Romans as undignified to her sex', and by putting it about a bit.

Meanwhile Augustus' stepson, Tiberius, decided he was fed up with holding important public positions in order to selflessly serve the state. He was also, most importantly, fed up with being married to Julia. He went on a career break/sulk to the island of Rhodes, much to Augustus' rage.

Julia's escapades soon became known to her father and she ended up banished to a much less nice island than Rhodes. Some years later her daughter (also named Julia) ended up being banished for much the same reasons (liking fun and hating weaving). Augustus was said to have declared: 'Would that I ne'er had wedded, and would I had died without offspring.'

1S7 ROMA. Museo Vaticano. Cesare Augusto.

One-man morality machine, Augustus Caesar.

Of course, it goes without saying (though we'll say it anyway), that Augustus was very far from the model of chastity himself. He was repeatedly unfaithful to his wife, Livia, and was said to enjoy deflowering girls well into his seventies.

What is the situation for women in Ancient Rome?

Women are expected to be chaste, loyal, dignified, modest and self-sacrificing. They are also expected to do a ton of weaving. Or at the very least sit at a loom pretending to weave whenever there are visitors.

Their main purpose in life is to produce children. This is why they are allotted no vote, no role in public office and a more limited role in the state religion. Rome needs an army and anything that could potentially limit the time available for pushing out future recruits is deemed very, very bad.

They also have to sit irritatingly far back at the Games. Though it's worth noting there is no such segregation at the chariot racing. The poet Ovid highly recommends the races as a great place to pick up girls, which might be of benefit or might make you wish for the sleaze-free, women-only seats in the amphitheatre.

The law also penalises women by insisting they have a guardian who oversees their financial affairs and generally pokes their nose in to check that they are being chaste, loyal, dignified, modest and self-sacrificing. Possibly he also runs his finger over the loom to check for dust.

The morality laws instituted under Augustus enshrined these traditionally held beliefs. Under these laws any woman caught committing adultery was subject to exile and her status reduced to that on a par with a prostitute, preventing her being able to remarry any Roman citizen. She was excluded from benefitting from any inheritance or legacies.

There are also penalties for being unmarried in the shape of an extra tax levied on both unmarried men and women.

DID YOU KNOW?

Adultery is only a crime in ancient Rome for women: men cannot be prosecuted for the same offence. A husband is obligated to divorce an unfaithful wife.

How to survive being a woman in Ancient Rome

Yes, my darlings, being a woman in ancient Rome can be restrictive. But it need not be too restrictive. I have some top tips on how to make your womanly life altogether not awful:

Get a slave, or maybe ten. Not only will it advertise your wealth and status to the neighbours, it'll also free up your time. While the slaves get on with the housework and weaving, you can nip out to the shops, the Games, the circus, or your lover's house.

Pop out three children or more. But really you only need to pop out three (four if you're a freedwoman). In an attempt to bolster the citizen birth rate, old emperor Augustus instituted rewards for women who have three children. The best of these rewards being you can ditch that pesky, nosey guardian for good!

Register as a prostitute. This might be a bit extreme, but it will allow you to enjoy passionate love affairs with whomever you wish without falling foul of adultery laws. A mega perk sadly unavailable to the daughters and granddaughters of equestrians and senators. Apparently, it was proving too tempting a loophole and dour, old spoilsport,

Lictors, protectors of the Vestal Virgins carrying their rods.

Tiberius, put an end to the wheeze pretty quickly. However, you plebeian ladies have no such restrictions.

Become a Vestal Virgin. There are great benefits to becoming a Vestal. Not only are you guardian free, you also get to sit on the front row at the games, unlike other women. Other benefits include your own team of lictors to bash annoying folk out the way; exceedingly handy in an overcrowded city like Rome. Best of all you are permitted to drive through Rome in a two-horse wagon, which is unbelievably handy and cool.

Choose the right type of marriage. Now, this is one I wish I'd got right for my first two marriages. In a manus marriage the bride passes from her father's family into that of her new husband. In a non-manus marriage a bride remains part of her father's family. A non-manus marriage makes an awful lot of sense. If your dear papa is lovely, why would you want to leave his caring protection? Plus, dear papa resides under his own roof, which means new hubby and you are free from his disapproving comments and control (most of the time). Also, if your papa remains your legal guardian, he can ensure your new in-laws are treating you to the lifestyle you expect, and will stop them from stealing all your money. On the other hand, should your papa not be dear and your other relatives' awful idiots, you might relish a chance to escape them by choosing a manus marriage.

For all the Roman romanticising of a woman's role, there are plenty of women unprepared to sit at home endlessly weaving underpants, breaking only to pop out another mini legionary. Though women visitors to Rome should be prepared for an awful lot of male whinging about everything they do.

Roman poet, Juvenal, moans incessantly about educated, cultured women who keep quoting poets he's never heard of. He's also thoroughly fed up with women at dinner parties making knowledgeable comparisons of Virgil and Homer. Not to mention those women initiating lawsuits and advising their consul on the technicalities of the law. How dare these uppity women know more than him.[4]

DID YOU KNOW?

Divorce is relatively simple in ancient Rome and can be initiated by men or women, though any children born of the marriage must stay with their father.

How are slaves treated?

Slavery is an everyday factor in Roman life which you will have to get used to. Though there is much hand wringing over the treatment of slaves, there is absolutely no discussion of abolition.

Slaves are subject to the whims of their masters or mistresses and have no legal rights. A slave's testimony in legal cases is only valid if extracted under torture. An assault or mugging on a slave is considered as damage to property. The slave owner can extract compensation for this damage, but the slave gets no recompense.

Slaves cannot legally marry. Any children born to them are the property of their master and they have no say over them. If the master decides to sell those children, they have no means to stop him.

Slaves are routinely physically punished by beatings and whippings. They have absolutely no autonomy over any aspect of their lives and live with the constant threat of being sold hanging over their heads.

If all that sounds a bit grim, you can at least console yourself that in 95 CE the lot of a slave has marginally improved from previous centuries.[5] Emperors have passed laws limiting the very worst abuses of slaves. For example, Claudius forbade owners from dumping their sick and elderly slaves once they were no longer useful. The current emperor, Domitian, has banned the castration of boys and fixed the price of the already 'de-balled', so that the slave traders can't cash in on a more limited supply of eunuchs.

DID YOU KNOW?

The Emperor Augustus had the legs of one of his slaves broken for divulging the content of a letter.

How you treat your slaves is seen very much to reflect on your character. The cultivated, enlightened slave owner need not use violence and will instead earn the respect of his workforce. Be overly harsh with your slave punishments and you may find yourself gaining some withering stares next time you're browsing through the Forum.[6]

However, the reverse is also true. How your slaves behave reflects on you. It's a difficult bar to balance on. Nobody wants to be seen as unnecessarily cruel, but similarly nobody wants to be the owner of arrogant and unruly slaves.

Will I own a slave?

If you want to show you have arrived in Rome then having a slave or slaves is a way to advertise that fact. Once one has reached a certain level of wealth you should definitely buy a slave. But make sure that you have enough money to feed an extra mouth and clothe your purchase respectably.

Slaves are very useful to have: they can keep your apartment clean and tidy, and you can send them out to the shops for supplies so you can stay in bed. If you have a bit of cash, you might want to invest in a literate slave because it's always nice to have a book read to you of an evening. A literate slave can also handle all the correspondence from irritating, nosey relatives.

A good time to buy a slave is after any military campaign when the market is flooded with captives. Some people prefer a *vernae* or home-bred slave, thinking them to be easier to train up and more docile and accepting of their status.

However, others find the northern barbarian lands produce hardy, hardworking slaves and prefer imported stock. Then there is always the flashy b****** who wants to show off their wealth by flaunting their exotic slave purchases from the distant east. Although everyone knows the climate in the east produces lazy, cowardly slaves.[7]

What about children?

Children are, of course, a bonus to any family – quite literally – for if you have three of them you get a tax break via the emperor's morality laws. Those of you with a large family will undoubtedly feel the invisible pleasure of the emperor beaming down on you at all times.

Contraception being somewhat limited in effectiveness means that you are quite likely to have some children at some point. On the upside, at a certain age children become useful. You can send them out on all the errands that you don't fancy doing. It's like having a slave, but without having to fork out coinage to some dubious trader whose words are as slippery as a lamprey eel. Also remember that it's perfectly acceptable to sign your child up for a bit of paid labour, which again makes them far more useful than a slave, who ultimately costs you money and earns you nothing in return.

However, like slaves, children can be extremely annoying. This is why when a baby is born it's worth taking a moment to decide whether it's worth rearing. Moodiness and obscene laziness are not terribly easy to distinguish in a newborn, so you are looking for other factors: chiefly whether the baby is fit and healthy.

Check that the baby's limbs move as expected, that it reacts to stimulus, that it cries immediately and vigorously, and that it is of a proper size and shape.[8] A sickly or disabled child, or worse, a girl,[9] is an additional cost that not every household can afford. It is therefore up to the *pater familias* to make the decision as to whether the baby is raised or exposed. If you decide upon exposure, the top place for leaving any unwanted baby is your nearest rubbish tip or cistern.

It should be stressed that exposure doesn't necessarily result in the death of the baby. Mythology is awash of stories of exposed infants rescued by kindly shepherds and raised as their own, before reaching adulthood and becoming embroiled in high adventure.

Admittedly, though, those adventures don't always turn out as well as they did for Rome's founder, and foundling, Romulus. Exposed infant Oedipus' family reunion went less than well when he killed his birth father and married his birth mother. Paris, who had been raised by a shepherd, had a no less extreme experience when he was reunited with his royal birth family: he brought about the destruction of his home city, Troy, and its entire civilisation.

One cannot blame any foundling for holding onto dreams of grandeur. Maybe it keeps them going through their most likely outcome, slavery. Exposed infants provided a good stream of slaves for the system.

How are children educated?

There are no designated school buildings in ancient Rome, teachers set up their classes wherever they can. This is often outside in the street, or under porticos (excellent cover for sudden rainstorms). Although this is a good way of enticing new pupils, by showing off how great a teacher you are for all to see, it is also pretty annoying for local residents who might fancy a bit of peace and quiet.

The best teachers are considered to be Greek, and not averse to physical violence, which is considered an excellent aid to learning. The children of the elite are more likely to be educated at home by one of their household slaves. An interesting exception to this is dour, old politician Cato the Elder. He decided to undertake the education of his son himself. He taught his son to read and write, and other skills such as horse riding. Given that one of the things he taught his son was how to swim across turbulent rivers, these lessons really don't sound much fun.

Later, to prepare them for public life, boys will be sent to an oratory school to learn the art of public speaking and the craft of coming up with really great insults for their political rivals. Any boy with an interest in philosophy might be sent to Greece to study the subject further, mainly because emperors have a habit of getting annoyed with philosophers and kicking them out of Rome.[10]

What if I don't want children, how can I prevent having them?

Family planning is very much practised in ancient Rome, and very successfully too, which is why successive emperors keep trying to bolster the birth rate with their irritating morality laws. There are a wide range of contraceptives available, such as:

- Boiled mule testicles mixed with the juice of the willow tree.
- Vulture dung.
- Rubbing juniper over the penis before intercourse.
- Squatting and sneezing after intercourse (for the woman).
- Wool soaked in honey/olive oil/crocodile dung placed in the vagina.

- Wearing part of a lioness's womb in an ivory tube.
- Cutting open the head of a particular hairy spider, in which you will find two small worms. These should be tied to the woman.

If these don't seem particularly appealing, or sexy, you might want to try a more reliable method of family planning; i.e., having sex with your slaves instead.[11]

Did the Romans have pets? Are they considered part of the family too?

Dogs are a Roman's best friend, and there are many memorial inscriptions to departed furry friends that prove this.

Other popular pets are birds and the imperial palace has its own aviary. It is the beloved hobby of any bird owner to teach their feathered pal to talk. There are varying successes at this. Empress Agrippina taught her pet thrush to talk, and ravens are given to speech, as are parrots. However, you are unlikely to get much out of a pigeon.

On the even stranger side, many Romans are extremely fond of their pet eels. Eel lovers are known to dedicate days of their lives to training their pets to come when called and feed from their hand. Some even adorn their slimy friends with fancy jewellery, such as necklaces and earrings.

So attached are Romans to their eels that they have been known to completely break down on their demise. We would recommend that you never mock the eel bereaved. It is grossly insensitive and cruel. Similarly, on visiting a friend's posh seaside home do find out where he stands on eels before ordering his chef to cook the contents of his garden pond for dinner.

DID YOU KNOW?

Wealthy Romans enjoyed creating vast indoor saltwater ponds stocked with all manner of sea creatures. Cicero sneeringly calls these hobbyists 'fish fanciers'.

Chapter 3

Clothing

What kinds of clothes would I wear?

This all depends on your gender, unless you're Caligula,[1] in which case feel free to take examples from both the following sections.

Men

The basis of any ancient Roman male's wardrobe is the tunic, a very simple garment consisting of a neck hole and two arm holes. They come with short sleeves for the summer or long sleeves for those cold Roman winters. The tunic may appear a bit samey, or even boring, but there are numerous ways to spruce up your tunic to stand out in the crowded Roman streets.

> **DID YOU KNOW?**
>
> Purple is made from the slime of sea snails. As it takes a lot of snails to produce a small amount of dye, it is ludicrously expensive.

Accessorise The most practical, and potentially stylish, accessory to the tunic is the belt. Wide or narrow, belted tight or loose, this can add a certain swagger to your tunic. It is also highly practical as loops can be added and useful implements/tools attached.

Colour Nobody said it had to be dull so get well and truly noticed with a vibrant shade. Alternatively, if you don't want to be noticed because your neighbourhood verges on the dodgy, then there are a wide variety of less vibrant colours to choose from.

Material Wool is cheapest, but why not try linen instead for a cooler, lighter feel? Or if you want to go all out, silk, though be prepared to be sneered at by traditionalists in the street who consider it effeminate and un-Roman. Also silk is super expensive, so you might want to touch up your local money lender for funds.

Length The most popular tunic variety is the knee length one. It is very practical as it doesn't drag in muddy puddles, or other questionable offerings on the streets of Rome. It also gives the opportunity to show off those nicely plucked legs. There's no point suffering the pain of the plucker if no one knows about it. For slaves you might want to cut their tunics a little shorter, particularly the more attractive ones; it'll drive your dinner guests crazy to look but not be able to touch.

Togas

You may believe that the toga is the standard outfit of the average Roman male, but you'd be very wrong. You are unlikely to see many togaed pedestrians on the streets of Rome, mainly because togas are formal wear, and are therefore only worn on certain festival days and very special occasions, but also because they are such an ungodly, fiddly item of clothing.

At their most basic the toga is a semi-circle of cloth of between 12 and 20ft that is draped about yourself and then over one arm. As togas are unfixed by anything handy, like a broach, they are liable to slip off, often at the most inopportune moment. They are, in short a pain, and it is a stoic Roman indeed who hasn't thrown the damn garment off screaming, 'I hate it. I absolutely hate it!'

The only folk you are likely to see wearing a toga are candidates standing for public office, because they are keen to express their very Roman-ness. It is also a test of their ability to perform under the pressure of a likely wardrobe malfunction. The clever candidate will employ a slave to look after his toga needs and prevent any embarrassing trips or rips.

Outerwear

A must have for your wardrobe is a cloak, which will protect you from the worst of Roman weather. For further warmth add a fur lining for that cosy feeling while out and about.[2] You can also accessorise your cloak with a broach, which handily doubles up as a weapon, should the need arise.

A brave toga wearer.

Footwear
It's sandals only. Top tip: it is permitted to wear socks with your sandals, and necessary in colder months. For a better grip choose sandals with nails in the soles.

DID YOU KNOW?

The Emperor Augustus veered towards shortness, so he had the soles of his sandals heightened to make him taller.

Underwear
A loin cloth may be wrapped about your nether region. Like the toga, this takes a certain skill to fix correctly in place. As a newcomer to the city, you might want to take advice on how to cloth up your loins properly, lest there be an embarrassing unravelling in the middle of the Forum.

Alternatively, woollen underpants are sometimes worn. Emperor Augustus was a big fan of them.[3] If that sounds a bit itchy and sweaty, there is the option of going pants-free. Though do remember that in a tunic there is a far greater chance of accidental flashing of parts that ought not to be seen, so watch out for any sudden movements or lunges.

Hair
The basic thing to remember about hair is: on head = good; anywhere else = not good.

Fashion dictates a smooth body to be most favourable, which will mean seeking out the services of the pluckers. They can be found at any decent bathhouse and for a small fee will remove any lurking hairs, wherever they may be. We'd advise asking around for a plucker with a smidgen of humanity. Sadly, sadists lurk in many professions.

If you can't face the agony of having your hairs pulled out one by one, there is always the alternative agony of having them singed off with red-hot walnut shells.

DID YOU KNOW?

The Emperor Otho shaved his chin every day and used moist bread to help prevent beard growth.

Hair on one's head is very important. To lose one's hair is considered a great grief that should avoided for as long as possible. The Emperor Otho resorted to a toupée that was so well made that nobody knew about it (except the historians who were still recording this fact seventy years later).

The current emperor, Domitian, has written a handy manual you might want to read, entitled: Care of the Hair.*

> The emperor is very sensitive about his own hair situation. I would very much recommend not mentioning anything about hair or loss of hair within a two mile radius of his Imperial Majesty. Though if you can find a way of praising his hairdressing manual without referencing his own deficiencies in that area that would very much please his Imperial Majesty.

DID YOU KNOW?

Romans believe bear grease mixed with extract of poppy prevents baldness. If you mix the bear grease with wine, it'll get rid of the dandruff from your preserved hair.

Women

Dresses

Roman women traditionally wear three layers of dress. First up is the tunic. Made of light material, this is a tube shape fixed at the shoulders. That fixing might be a simple sewn seam or perhaps buttons or clasps. It's a very versatile garment and can be infuriatingly modest or suggestively draped.

Over the top of this ankle-length tunic is the *stola,* or outer dress. The *stola* is the standard wear for all respectable women. It is usually a woollen garment, held together with broaches, or *fibulae* as they are known. It can be belted beneath the bustline with long or short sleeves, depending on the season.

The final layer is the *palla,* or shawl. This is not fixed but rather draped round the body and over an arm, much like a toga, and is no doubt as annoyingly slippy as that garment. It also doubles as a veil covering the hair for that extra pious look.

Suggestions for lady wear.

The joy of having three layers is that they can be of three different colours and will really make you stand out. Unless of course you don't want to stand out because you're trying to escape from somewhere you shouldn't be without being spotted, in which case we'd recommend you coordinate in a dull grey colour and keep that *palla* pulled down.

Underwear
In this era underwear hasn't got sexy. The best on offer is a breast band, which can either flatten or prop 'em up, depending on your mood.

The benefits of the three layers become clear when it comes to pants: you don't have to wear them and, unlike those poor short-tunic-wearing men, you can lounge about all over the place with no concerns as to your modesty. Leather-style bikini briefs are, however, available for exercise and/or acrobatic acts.

Footwear
Sandals or (joy) flip flops.

Hair
Great news, ladies, the Flavian era is the era of big hair. Really BIG hair. With no hairspray or gel, these towering edifices of curls are the work of a specialist hairdresser, known as an *ornatrix*. These are fabulously talented, very much in-demand, and thus expensive, slaves. The tools of their trade are enough hair pins to arm a legion and heated curling tongs. Along with a tough skin needed to withstand the demanding nature of their mistresses. These hairstyles take hours to perfect, so be prepared for a long sit as the *ornatrix* busies arounds you.[4]

Flavian lady hair: the biggest and the best.

If you want something a bit less demanding, less showy and less likely to blow over in windy weather you could try a simple bun style. It's classic, it's easy and it comes cheap as you can do it yourself.

DID YOU KNOW?

The Romans believed that having your hair cut on the seventeenth or twenty-ninth of the month prevented both hair loss and headaches.

Accessories
Whilst the men are left to mess about with their belts, women can adorn themselves in a multitude of ways. Hair can be enlivened by pins, clips, headbands or even, if you're feeling particularly fancy, a tiara.

Jewellery-wise there are necklaces, earrings, rings and bangles; the whole jingly shebang. Empress to Caligula, Lollia Paullina, once turned up to dinner in 40 million sesterces worth of pearls! Though do bear in mind she had the entire Praetorian guard to protect her and her jewels.

My Beauty Routine: Hortensia

I cannot overemphasize how important a good beauty routine is for a Roman lady. Not only because the city is full to bursting with beautiful women (or the competition, as I call them) but also because being excluded from most of public life means you have a lot of hours to fill not serving the state/serving in the army/making up amusing but cruel insults for your political enemies.

First up, skin. A soft, squishy unmarked skin is essential to show off that you are rich enough not to work. Not working frees up your time to soak in asses' milk. This will make your skin brilliantly soft to the touch. Top tip: only fresh milk, darlings. Trust me, the sour variety will linger like anything. Nobody wants to be the source of that bad smell at the top dinner party of the season.

White, pale skin is the prettiest and most valued. Nobody wants to look like they've spent the day in the fields pulling crops. This is why you simply must remember a sun hat when you go to the Games, particularly if you have one of those disapproving husbands who thinks wives should be looming it all day. As if!

A red face is a dead giveaway you've been outdoors. So, darlings, sun hats and Hortensia's secret face powder. Admittedly I had to ask my slave girl what's in it. She tells me: barley, pea plants, narcissus bulbs, gum, spelt, honey and the ground-up horn of a lusty stag. She informs me it simply has to be a lusty stag, no other will do. Which does make me worry how the poor dear is spending her days.

I can vouch that it does give the skin a magnificent white countenance. I know there are those who recommend white lead, but I have never liked it.[5]

On top of this I may add a little red to my cheeks and my lips. My slave girl tells me she prefers to use poppies all mashed together, but says something about ochre being dead expensive. Whatever ochre is.[6]

People, and by people I mean men, often tell me that my eyes are my best feature. So I make sure I accentuate their translucent beauty with a line of black kohl on the lids and a smudge of green malachite[7] above.

With my face done I dunk myself in enough perfume to alert passers-by that I can afford the ridiculously over-the-top expensive Arabian variety. Then I'm ready to go! And sit for the morning while *ornatrix* works her wonders. I find that some decent reading material, a wine skin of Falerian and my favourite gossipy slave help pass the time.

What do children wear?

Pretty much the same as the grown-ups, except in a smaller size. Boys will wear a tunic. Girls, the ankle-length dress also worn by their mothers. Both sexes wear protective amulets until they reach the safety of adulthood. Boys wear a pouch, generally constructed out of leather (though the children of the wealthy may sport the more pimped-up gold version) on a chain round their neck. Known as a *bulla*, this contains objects that are considered lucky and that will protect the boy until he reaches manhood.

When the boy comes of age he removes his *bulla* and dedicates it to his household gods, the Lares. He will then don the *toga virilis*[8] to show that he is now a Roman male.

Girls wear the *lunula*, which is crescent shaped, and considered to hold similar protective powers to the *bulla*.

DID YOU KNOW?

The *toga picta* was reserved for triumphant generals. It was dyed entirely purple and decorated with gold thread.

How will I wash my clothes?

You could follow the example of the Emperor Nero and never wear the same garment twice. But failing the riches of an emperor, you will have to visit the laundry. There is generally one on most streets in Rome and you'll easily find it by following the smell, for the standard way to wash clothes is in vast vats of stale urine. Top tip, if you want to earn an extra ass or two, laundries are always in need of a quick top-up of their washing product so why not offer your wee for sale rather than hunt down a public latrine.

Chapter 4

Accommodation

One of the most important aspects of your visit in ancient Rome will be where to stay. As a stranger to the city you are at a disadvantage in lacking any connections who could put you up for the duration of your stay. We shall guide you through your options.

What sort of accommodation does Rome offer?

If you're picturing a massive villa with mosaic floors, frescoed walls and probably some kind of cool water feature, you might want to adjust your expectations slightly. Most people in Rome live in apartment blocks called *insula*. These are between three and eight stories tall and are usually rented rather than owned.

There are 30,000 such blocks of *insula* in Rome, which at least gives you plenty of options. Apartments can be rented long term or even by the day if you fancy a short stay. Look out for notices of available abodes scrawled onto the walls of the city, such as this example from Pompeii:

> The city block of the Arrii Pollii in the possession of Gnaeus Alleius Nigidius Maius is available to rent from July 1st. There are shops on the first floor, upper stories, high-class rooms and a house. A person interested in renting this property should contact Primus, the slave of Gnaeus Alleius Nigidius Maius.

What should I consider when choosing an apartment?

Cost
Roman accommodation is expensive. Moaning about this is a very Roman pastime, so do join in complaints that a small hovel in the city

these days is the same price as a generous villa in the countryside. Alongside this, share dreams of escaping Rome to some peaceful seaside resort for a tenth of the price, or of owning a farm of your own in the beautiful countryside. Importantly, you must never actually do these things. Because Rome is the greatest city of them all and nobody would voluntarily leave her stinking, crowded, dirty streets.

With a large and ever-growing population, the buildings are packed in tightly, so expect to find your neighbours close by. Very close by. You'll probably be able to shake hands through your windows. Though on the upside such close proximity to your neighbours means you'll be able to store up a good stash of Rome's favourite pastime, gossip.[1]

The most expensive apartments are on the first floor. As most blocks have shops on the ground floor, it is essential to check which businesses are in the vicinity. Advisor to Nero, Seneca, really should have checked before moving into his apartment. It overlooked a bathhouse and he was driven quite mad by the noise of the grunts of the weightlifters, the slapping of the masseur's hands and the shrieking of those suffering from the hair plucker's trade.[2]

Unless you like to party all night, we'd suggest avoiding living above a cookshop, despite how lovely the smell of bubbling food might be. These are popular hangouts for gamblers and all manner of groups of people bent on causing trouble.[3] Perhaps an apartment above a nice clothing shop or a pots and pans retailer would be a good option.

Amenities
Your apartment will not have a toilet. Or running water. Or likely any cooking facilities. Most Romans take their grain to the bakers to be made into bread for them and visit local takeaway food shops.

For that other bodily process, we recommend a chamber pot. If you are on the top floor, though, you might want to have several to save yourself walking down six flights of stairs to empty them.

It should be noted that public toilets are a common feature of Rome and, like the bakers and takeaways, a good communal spot to pick up gossip and engage in social discourse. Also, to laugh at a fellow's bowel discomfort.

Fire and building collapses

Now you are settled comfortably in your new home we need to go through some of the dangers to look out for. Don't look so worried, there is no need to panic. Relax. Sit back. Though maybe take notes, because the following might just save your life.

Neither is particularly rare in Rome, sadly. Though the fire under Nero was infamous enough to gain the epithet of 'great', it is far from alone in its devastation. There was a fire under the rule of Titus, older brother to the current emperor, that ran unchecked for three days and three nights.

This is where that first-floor apartment comes in handy should you need to make a hasty exit. Rome does have its own team of firefighters called the Vigiles. Prior to this, crafty politician Crassus had assembled his own team of 500 firefighters who would rush to the scene of the blaze, then stand by and watch it burn while they waited for payment from the fleeing residents before intervening. This is how Crassus became so very rich.

Building regulations are thin on the ground, as are town planners. This is handy for the rapid erection of much needed housing for Rome's ever-growing population. It's less good for producing safe accommodation. The Emperor Augustus limited the height of blocks to under seventy feet, but haphazard buildings are part and parcel of living in Rome.

'Most of Rome is propped up with planks to stop it falling down,' comments the poet, Juvenal, dryly. Even Cicero, who presumably could afford a decent block, complained that two of his invested rental properties had collapsed.

You are thus forewarned that at the first rumble you should leg it down the stairs. Don't worry about the embarrassment should it turn out to be thunder or a passing cart. It is better to be safe than dead.

What are the homes of the rich like?

The fanciest of fancy villas is naturally that belonging to the emperor. This is situated on the Palatine Hill. In the Republican era the Palatine was a desirable place to live, but these days private dwellings are rare as the imperial family have slowly taken over the whole hill.

The general rule of thumb is that the higher up the hill, the larger the house. The valleys at the bottom tend to be the slum areas, most noticeably the Subura in the Esquiline district of Rome. Elsewhere on the Esquiline you will find some pleasant public gardens and some very grand homes.

The homes of rich Romans are, naturally, better than those of the poor. Not least because they have indoor plumbing, which means not only is there underfloor heating for those chilly winter mornings but also bathrooms with running water!

DID YOU KNOW?

Sergius Orata made his fortune by inventing the shower-bath. The ingenious Orata was also the first to develop oyster farming.

Roman houses face inwards to protect the owner's privacy and to insulate against the noisy streets outside, with the public rooms being towards the street and the private rooms further back into the house. The elite Roman house is both a public and a private space. Your average Roman will chat to his friends and conduct business on the street whereas the elite Roman invites them into his house in order to show off just how important he is.

Architect Vitruvius recommends men in public office have a home that contains libraries and oblong meeting rooms, to enable them to fulfil their public office. It is important that the elite homeowner personally supervises which books are available in his library. His slaves may have very different takes on what literature is appropriate for a man of his standing. It could be very embarrassing should a copy of, say, *Ovid* be found in his collection by a visiting official or even one of his clients.[4]

The atrium is always the first room entered, so it needs to be suitably impressive for any visitors. There is a practical need for a large atrium, for it is here that patrons will gather their clients each morning. Many patrons will install an imposingly massive chair in their atrium to sit on while their clients queue up to offer their services or ask for a favours. The very richest have enough clients to form a decent mob: something that was a standard tactic during the Republican era but less needed in these, calmer, emperor-ruling days.

The standard atrium decoration is a display of the busts and/or death masks of the owner's ancestors. This signifies to all those who enter both the pedigree and importance of the owner. Atriums can be fancied up with a small pond which serves as a useful cooling feature in summer and a reliable form of entertainment as guests accidentally step/fall into it.

Given the amount of entertaining an elite Roman is expected to do, a swanky dining room is a must-have. Perhaps one with channels between the couches in which lamps or dishes of food can be floated. Or perhaps there might be a rotating ceiling that guests can lie back and admire.[5] Some houses even have walls that squirt a pleasant perfume

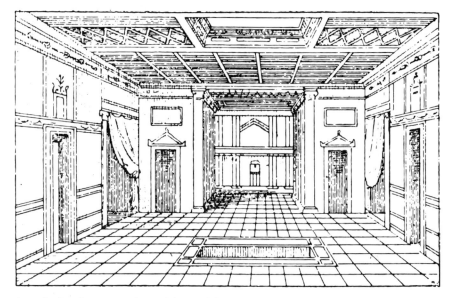

A typical atrium, complete with pond for accidentally stepping in.

onto guests: a necessity for the dutiful patron who is required to invite all his clients to dine at some point (even the grubby ones).

All Roman homes, swanky or otherwise, will have a shrine to the Lares, the household gods. This needs daily attention, otherwise the arm might fall off that fancy Greek statue you got in Corinth. Or something terribly might happen to your family, though they are thankfully more easily replaceable, particularly the slaves.

DID YOU KNOW?

As well as using mosaics to decorate floors, Romans also used them on their ceilings too.

As well as a house in Rome, all elite families will have at least one other home. The bay of Naples is a particularly popular spot for a villa, with the town of Baiae much favoured. Baiae has acquired a reputation for debauchery and decadence (that is, fun). As Varro puts it, Baiae is, 'The place where old men come to become young boys again and young boys come to become young girls.'

The benefit of an out of town house is that you are not so constrained by space. Pliny the Younger's out of town house in Laurentum comprised a gymnasium, a heated swimming pool, a ball court, two dining rooms, bathrooms, a terrace and covered arcade. A house by the coast might easily have ninety separate rooms, including the essential chamber with the sea view.

How are the homes of the rich decorated?
Throw out any thoughts of magnolia, the Romans didn't go in for muted colour schemes. They went bold or rather **bold**. Colour is definitely very much in. Reds, blacks and gold are to be found on the walls of the homes of Rome's wealthier classes. If you think that might be a bit headache inducing, remember that Romans lacked electricity and they didn't go in for huge expansive windows. Bright colours enhanced the dim light available from lamps.

The theme of the interior decor must fit with the image the owner is trying to project. Common motifs in frescos include scenes of animals, such as crocodiles, hippos and lions, still lives of fruit and other foods, and garden scenes that transplant the outside inside, with birds perching on lush green foliage. Also mythological scenes, such as Narcissus falling in love with his own reflection,[6] the Trojan war or Leda having it away with a swan, feature heavily.

There are also those scenes that may appear lurid to the modern visitors, such as depictions of Priapus with his grotesquely large erect penis. Don't be alarmed by such images, Priapus is a god associated with fertility and plentiful food. You are permitted to be slightly alarmed by frescoes depicting bountiful copulating couples, since it's possible you might have accidentally wandered into a brothel.

A very popular style is to divide the space with painted columns so well rendered as to seem three dimensional. Added to the illusion are vases and other ornaments placed on top of these deceptively real pillars, which is handy because it cuts down on the need for actual vases and ornaments.

DID YOU KNOW?

Frescoes are created by painting onto wet plaster. Fresco means 'fresh'.

An example of interior design from Pompeii.

Floor designs need to be as carefully thought out as the walls. Mosaics come in all manner of designs, from simple, but very effective, geometric patterns to elaborate representations of gladiators, animals or even the discarded food from a banquet. The aim again is to announce what sort of person you are to all visitors (answer: a very rich one), with a mosaic floor coveted over any neighbour's ass, no matter how fine.

In terms of interior design, impressive statues are also a must-have feature. Greek art is considered the most sophisticated. Handily, the Roman conquest of Greece and Emperor Nero's tour of that province has meant there is a large amount of purloined Greek art floating around to fill the villas of the rich.

DID YOU KNOW?

Nero's golden house had a dining room with a running waterfall in it. Perfect for keeping his guests cool during summer.

The emperor's holiday house

His Imperial Majesty's most favourite home is set high in the Alban hills, only ten miles from Rome. It has some wonderful terraces overlooking Lake Alba, along which the emperor likes to stroll on his private post-dinner walk.[7] Situated up high there is a lovely cooling breeze, even in the hottest of months.

A theatre provides entertainment for his Imperial Majesty to enjoy performances of the great plays of our day. The grounds also house a substantial hippodrome where the emperor can enjoy chariot races.

But the emperor's most favourite pastime, and one in which he excels in, is archery. His skill is such that he can fire arrows into a moving beast that are in the exact place that horns would be. He has been known to despatch over a hundred creatures in a single day. This has caused some anguish for us staff since the area was soon depleted of animals for his Imperial Majesty to hunt, which has meant we have to cart them over from Rome in sufficient numbers for one of the emperor's stays.

Should there be any mess-up in these arrangements I make sure the weak link in the chain is volunteered for the emperor's other favourite party trick: firing arrows through the splayed fingers of a slave.

An imperial garden, on the Palatine Hill.

Chapter 5

Shopping

Where can I buy food and other items?

For food, the best and freshest produce is available at the *nundinae*. These are the markets that are held every nine days. As wagons are not allowed in the city during the day, farmers will travel with their goods overnight and set up at dawn.

A top tip is to get to the market as close to dawn as possible. Given that Romans count the day from the first hour of light, this is not as ridiculously early as you might think. It's also in your best interest to get to market before hundreds of Roman housewives squeeze that cheese you really fancy for your dinner into an off-putting shape.

If you can't take the brutal competition for goods, maybe try shopping at one of the permanent markets and shops. A good place to start is at one of the forums. A forum is a multi-purpose space for shopping, pleasing the gods, defending yourself in court, showing off a bit and catching up with all the gossip.

The Forum
There are several forums in Rome and the original and the best needs no additional name to distinguish it. Say you are going to the forum and nobody will ask which one. This public space was created by the kings of Rome and has been added to ever since, which accounts for the jumble of buildings.

There is so much of importance and interest to see here that we'd recommend having a good explore before you immerse yourself in retail therapy. Notable buildings include the Senate House, where laws are made, and the Basilica Julia, where those laws are enacted in the standing courts. Also look out for the rostra, this is a long, flat rectangular platform used for public speaking. It gets its name from the points of ships (or rostrum) that decorate it.

The rostra has born witness to many famous events, including that rousing speech by Mark Antony that begins, 'Friends, Romans, Countrymen, lend me your ears.'[1] They did lend their ears to Mark Antony, who roused them into a fiery mob and Brutus' house spontaneously burnt down. A similar thing happened when ex-tribune of the plebs, Publius Clodius, was assassinated. Clodius' body was carried by supporters and laid on the rostra, which roused the plebs into another fiery mob. This time the Senate House spontaneously burnt down.[2]

Other key, less fiery events that have taken place on the rostra include Augustus' daughter, Julia, allegedly using it to tout for sexual partners, Mark Antony, pre-rousing speech days, puking up his guts all over it,[3] and its use as a general repository for the assorted body parts of dead enemies of the state.[4]

In a nutshell, if it's all going to kick off, the rostra is the place it'll kick off from. Which makes it a good place to loiter before hitting the shops.

DID YOU KNOW?

Before the Flavian Amphitheatre was built gladiator bouts and wild beast hunts were held in the Forum.

The Forum is home to many temples, which comes in handy for getting the gods on your side before a spot of bargain hunting. The Temple of Concordia, the goddess of agreements, might be a good bet for the price haggling to come. Don't miss out on visiting the unusually circular Temple of Vesta and checking that the Vestals haven't let the sacred flame go out.[5]

There's the chance to show appreciation to the emperor's father at the Temple of Vespasian. Also be sure to go and see the Arch of Titus, which was built by Domitian to commemorate his brother's successful campaigning in Judaea. It's also a handy space to stand under if it rains.

Head down to the far end of the Forum, near the Capitoline Hill, and you will find the Tarpeian Rock. If you're lucky it might be an execution day and you can watch a felon be pushed from its summit into the Forum below.

On a similar theme, the nearby Gemonian stairs are traditionally where the bodies of traitors are placed, so everyone can give them a good kicking. It was here that Tiberius' duplicitous Prefect ended up.

Also, more recently, Vitellius was led through the streets of Rome and killed here in 69 CE.

Once you've had a good dose of culture Roman style, you'll be ready for that shopping. The place to head to is the Via Sacre, the road which runs through the Forum from the Capitoline Hill to the Flavian Amphitheatre. The Via Sacre is Rome's exclusive shopping district, so expect to find exclusive items at eye-watering prices: think jewellery, perfume, spices and other luxury goods.

DID YOU KNOW?

On the Via Sacre is a shop that sells garments decorated with gold. It's run by lady entrepreneur, Selia Epyre.

Imperial Forums

The Forum, unsurprisingly given the amount of activities that go on, is extremely busy and crowded. Successive emperors have endeavoured to make it altogether less appealing by building their own forums in order to draw away the crowds. There are to date, three imperial Forums: the Forum of Julius Caesar; the Forum of Augustus; the Forum of Domitian.[6]

DID YOU KNOW?

To purchase the land for the Forum of Julius Caesar cost sixty million sesterces.

All of these forums have lines of shops to browse through. The Argiletum area near the new Forum of Domitian is the place to head to for book lovers. Here you will find many shops selling the latest scrolls. The Forum of Domitian is also the home to a huge statue of the emperor sitting on a horse, which Roman (suck-up) court poet, Statius, dedicates many, many verses to saying how wonderful it is.[7] It would, therefore, be rude to miss it.

Other things worth seeing are the mighty Temple of Mars Ultor, in the Forum of Augustus, and the gold statue of Cleopatra in the Temple of Venus, in the Forum of Julius Caesar. As Caesar dedicated this temple himself and chose the statutes personally, we can assume it is a good likeness.

Other places to shop are: Forum Holitorium, for all your vegetable needs; Forum Boarium, which has a regular cattle market; and Saepta Julia, if you're in the mood for buying slaves.

Best buys

Hello, darlings. Sometimes with so much on offer in Rome it can be most taxing making a decision on your purchases. But don't worry, my dears, I am here to tell you what's hot and what should really be avoided at all costs.

Firstly, fresh produce should always be local. The more local, the better. Yes, Egypt is terribly civilised and chic, but I really cannot vouch for how that fruit basket has survived the journey.[8]

Olive oil, always Italian. We produce the best variety, which is why we export it all over the empire, and beyond.

The best figs come from Africa. Accept no smaller, less juicy versions. Also coming from Africa are those grain ships that keep Romans fed.[9]

There is only one place to get your frankincense and that is Arabia. Accept no other, because it's a con, as I, sadly, once discovered myself. Arabia is also where to get your myrrh from. Like frankincense, they've had to add an extra harvest each year to meet Roman demands, and still it is harder to find than an honest politician.

If balsam is your scent, then the only place to get that is from Judaea. Other superior scents can be purchased from Delos, Athens and Egypt. The more exotic the scent, the more expensive. But that, of course is the idea, my darlings. We women of Rome have to show our material worth in more subtle ways than the men. We can't put on Games or throw money at the plebs. We must display our wealth in other ways.

If we are talking wealth displays, we simply must talk about jewellery. Spain is by far the biggest producer of gold. Which is why you shouldn't purchase it, it's so very common. What is less common is Indian gold. I am told that it is collected up by ants.[10]

To accompany your gold, you may wish to add pearls. But darlings, I find the fashion for pearls has made them all too ordinary and nobody wants to be ordinary. I prefer an Ethiopian sapphire or

---

an emerald from Arabia. One should adorn oneself with the products of all the empire. Although I know of some terribly grumpy sorts who claim that imported goods have ruined Rome. They, of course, know nothing and if only they would slip on the finest Chinese silk, I feel sure they would instantly change their minds.

DID YOU KNOW?

Arabian perfume is sprinkled on the pyre at funerals. When Empress Poppaea died, Nero poured more perfume on her pyre than Arabia produces in a whole year.

Buying slaves

Purchasing new slaves can be very stressful. How can you be sure that your purchase will put the effort in? Will he/she be a disruptive influence on your other slaves? Is the purchase strong and hardy? Don't fret, for here are our top tips on buying slaves.

Nationality
This needs careful consideration. Peoples born in different climates have differing personality traits.[11] Those born in warm, eastern climates are easier to manage, whereas those from the cold north are more fiercely independent. However, the latter are much braver, which may suit if you are looking for a heavy to menace your debtors.

Fashion dictates that secretaries and doctors be of Greek origin. Similarly, there is a craze for bathroom attendants to be of Ethiopian[12] appearance. The more exotic looking the slave, the more social capital for the owner, for Romans love anything a little bit out of the ordinary.[13]

Special traits
As noted, Romans love an oddity and it's worth having at least one in your stock to whip out at dinner parties. Mark Antony, for instance, paid 200,000 for a set of twins. Admittedly it turned out they weren't twins but merely two men who looked alike, but still. The current emperor,

Domitian, has banned the castration of boys, so that eunuch you have polishing your sandals has now increased in rarity. Time to put him back on front-of-house duties.

Other special traits involve useful stuff like literacy or being a trained architect or accountant.

Captured or vernae?
Another important question to think about before purchasing is whether you'd prefer a *vernae* slave, that is, one born in slavery, or one newly captured and enslaved. The latter may well be more troublesome, being unused to their new status. But then again that might make them more malleable, being traumatised by recent experiences. Your *vernae* slave may be fully stuck in their ways as to what being a slave involves. They may also unfairly compare you with their previous owner and find you lacking. Nobody needs that kind of crushing criticism in their own home.

Health
This is an important one to check before you hand over any money, because if your new purchase dies in your house, the slave trader is very much going to say it's your fault and refuse to refund your money.

Check every part of their anatomy, even the tongue, because it's useful to have one if they're going to be an announcer. Plus, be sure to examine their back. A plethora of whip scars could denote a very troublesome slave.

Mental health can be harder to determine but the law does state you should be told if the slave had previously contemplated suicide or had run away.

But most of all, remember this: all slave traders are liars.

DID YOU KNOW?

Caligula's personal bodyguards were all Germans.

Chapter 6

Food and Diet

What kind of food did the Romans have access to?

It's probably easier to list the foods the Romans didn't have, rather than what they did:

- No tomatoes
- No pasta
- No chocolate
- No potatoes

You may well now be lamenting a life bereft of spaghetti Bolognese, comforting piles of mashed potatoes and energy-boosting Mars Bars, but honestly, it's not all bad. The Romans have a wide variety of food available to them, not least because of the size of their empire from which they can import food. The Emperor Vitellius took advantage of this when he created a dish he named, 'The Shield of Minerva', which consisted of ingredients from 'every corner of the Empire right from the Parthian frontier to the Spanish Straits.'[1]

Meats the Romans eat include hare, boar, lamb, wild goat, pork, venison and veal. Fancy a roast bird? You could try partridge, pigeon, pheasant, goose or chicken. If you are feeling a bit exotic maybe have an ostrich or a peacock, though we'd recommend saving these for a posh dinner party. There's no point flaunting your wealth to your household slaves after all.

As the Romans are an empire based around the Mediterranean, fish and sea food are plentiful. A recipe book from the first century CE includes meals comprised of ray, calamari, cuttlefish, oysters, mussels, sardines and sea urchins.

Lamprey eels doubled as food and a quick way of getting rid of your useless slaves. A certain Vedius Pollo claimed it was only way he had of watching a man be torn to pieces, which was apparently how Pollo liked to pass his time. Lovely man.

DID YOU KNOW?

Fish were highly prized in ancient Rome with one man paying 8,000 sesterces for a single fish!

There are few surprises in the fruits and vegetable available. These include beets, leeks, lentils, peas, chestnuts, beans, chickpeas, grapes, pomegranates, figs, apples, pears, peaches, olives, cabbage and mushrooms, most of which can be pickled and stored for consumption out of season.

The Romans are big on sauces, and most particularly garum. This is the sauce of choice, and if you want to truly fit in, we'd recommend you dab it on everything while loudly declaiming that the pure mackerel version is the best. For your own benefit it's probably best not to know how garum is produced. But if you are very, very sure you want to know: 'The entrails of fish are placed in a vat and salted – Salt the whole mixture and place it in the sun. After it has aged in the heat.'[2]

Yes, garum, the ketchup of the ancient world, is effectively rotting fermenting fish entrails. Tuck in!

Apicius' Cookbook

Top Roman foodie, Marcus Gavius Apicius, wrote a recipe book in the first century CE that offers quite an insight into what foods and tastes the ancient Romans enjoyed.

The temptation with Apicius is to pull out the most extravagant and jaw-dropping recipes and have a good marvel. Let us give into temptation and delve into the more unusual meals he suggests.

Flamingos

I'm willing to bet that nobody in the twenty-first century has ever gazed upon a flock of neon-pink flamingos and thought, 'Mmm, Sunday lunch.' However, the ancient Roman flamingo was a delicacy

---

that could be served multiple ways. Their tongues were said to be of the most exquisite flavour.

Apicius suggests roasting flamingo with pepper, parsley, mint, dates, honey, wine, vinegar and oil. They could also be boiled with a smattering of leeks and coriander. Given that flamingos can be as tall as five feet you have to wonder how big the pot was and what happened to those long flamingo legs. But don't panic if you can't face hacking off stringy pink limbs, because Apicius tells us that these recipes work just as well for parrots.

Flamingos. Yum.

Dormouse
Kitchen too small to prep flamingo? Allergic to feathers and can't try the parrot alternative? Why not try dormice instead? Apicius suggests stuffing them with pork, pepper and nuts. This can be officially classed as fiddly.[3]

Snails
Beloved by our Gallic cousins today, snails were also served up in ancient Rome. Apicius recommends prepping them for maximum flavour by serving up your snails a dish of milk. Make sure you add more milk to their dish each day and pay close attention. You are waiting for the exact moment your snails are too fat to fit in their shells. This is when you should strike and fry them in oil. It probably helps not to become too attached to the snails.

Further suggestions
If covering your apartment in pink feathers, extreme dormouse dexterity, or pan-frying your pet snails doesn't appeal, then how about some asparagus custard or splayed sow's womb.

51

What did the poor eat?

Fair enough. We've listed food that is around, but it isn't necessary available to every Roman. Particularly when people are prepared to pay more for a fish than it would cost to buy the fisherman, his boat and his favourite fishing net.

The poor receive a grain dole, which they can take to a local baker to produce a loaf for them, as most accommodation in Rome does not include kitchen facilities. It's a good way to get to know the neighbours as you all hang out together waiting for your bread to bake. Aside from bread, the diet of the poor is enlivened by a bit of sausage or cheese or perhaps vegetables.

As few have kitchens it's handy that Rome is awash with cookshops for eating in or taking away. They are not just for the poor. The Emperor Claudius declared his fondness for taverns, saying 'But I ask, my lords, how can anyone live without an occasional snack?'[4] Who indeed, your Imperial Majesty?

Be sure to add your restaurant review on the wall outside, such as this one from Herculaneum: 'Two friends were here. While they were, they had bad service in every way from a guy named Epaphroditus. They threw him out and spent 105 and half sestertii most agreeably on whores.'[5]

A takeaway from Pompeii. The round holes held pots of bubbling food.

DID YOU KNOW?

Many religious festivals in Rome involve animal sacrifices. There is then often a banquet afterwards where the meat is dished out for all to enjoy.

What do wealthy Romans eat?

Whatever they like, and to show off that they are obscenely wealthy they will think nothing of drinking the most expensive of perfumes (in the belief it will make them smell as sweet on the inside as the out[6]). See also dissolving pearls in vinegar and drinking the mixture, as Cleopatra is said to have done.[7]

The best place to sample the finest and richest of Roman food is at a private dinner party. Securing an invitation, however, is not for the faint-hearted. There is no sitting back expecting them to come to you. Similarly, just because you invited someone to your party doesn't mean you will receive reciprocation. You need to go forth and earn your invitation. This takes persistence, guile and borderline stalking.

How to secure a dinner party invitation

My former husband, the second one (we must never speak of the first, darling), was a shameless social climber. Mostly because he was so very inconveniently poor and hoped that some wealthy, aged and childless senator would take a fancy to him and adopt him into the family fortune.

It was I that suggested a good way to meet his future papa was to attend all the best dinner parties, portraying the right mix of budding potential and son-appeal. We had firstly to obtain the necessary invitations. Gate-crashing is so not the done thing, my darling. My top three tips are:

Persistence is a virtue
Turn up at your proposed host's morning client session, turn up at their public speech and cheer them on, turn up at dinner time.

Repeat every day and they will soon be sick enough of the sight of you to invite you to their party for a sole night.[8]

Hang around the baths
Not only is it a useful place to show how witty and entertaining a party guest you'll be, but also certain notable hosts are known to issue invitations based on what they see beneath the water line. This obviously means a regular gym routine, but do remember not to approach your target in the cold pool; it's most limiting to your assets.

Be an appalling suck up
Leave your dignity at the door and act out the role of the perfect client. Do everything and more that your potential host asks you. Laugh at his appalling jokes, compliment his ugly wife, shower him with services and freebies.

Important caveat here: make sure the dinner is worth your efforts. Rome is full of truly awful dinner parties where the host inflicts their awful poetry on you, or shamefully saves all the best food for themselves and the lesser cuts for their guests. Life is really too short to suffer an insufferable host.

DID YOU KNOW?

The poet Martial knew of a man who hung round the public latrines all day in the hope of securing a dinner party invitation.

What should I expect at a dinner party?

Dinner parties are as varied as their hosts. At an imperial dinner party one should expect the unexpected. Maybe even a spot of murder. It was at one of Nero's dinner parties that his stepbrother, Britannicus, was poisoned. Caligula was fond of inviting couples to his parties and then selecting the most attractive wife for himself. Otho's intimate party of close friends was interrupted when the Praetorian guard stormed his banquet thinking the emperor was in danger. He wasn't, but his guests certainly were, with the heavily armed soldiers mowing them down between courses.

DID YOU KNOW?

The Emperor Claudius made it lawful to break wind at a dinner party, both 'quietly or noisily'.[9]

The current emperor, Domitian, held a black banquet. The guests arrived to find their surroundings entirely black: the walls, the floor, the ceiling. They were settled on black-draped couches beside slabs of stone in the shape of gravestones. They were served black-coloured food in black dishes by slaves entirely naked and painted, yes you've guessed it, black. Quite unsurprisingly the guests were somewhat unnerved by this theme and one suspects the small talk was of a rather forced kind.

In more general terms you should expect food and entertainment of a sort. One key thing to remember is that at a posh dinner party you are expected to dine reclined. By reclined, we mean lying on your left side, freeing up your right hand to eat with.

Couches have three sides, with a table placed in the middle. Be prepared to be sociable, since you will be sharing your couch with up to nine other diners. The quality of your couch sharers will signify where you stand in your host's affection. This can be quite dispiriting, but some loudly aired, witty conversation might alert your host that you are worthy of an upgrade. Alternatively, he may decide you're a loud bore and never invite you to dine again.

What kind of food will be served?

For the most extravagant hosts, it's a case of Apicius' entire cookbook gone mad. Vitellius' Shield of Minerva dish mentioned earlier included ingredients such as: 'the livers of pike, the brains of pheasants and peacocks, the tongues of flamingos and the milt of lampreys.'[10] If you're wondering what 'milt' is, it's semen. The semen of eels. Which is nearly almost appetising in a line-up that includes peacock brains.

Other 'treats' include the notorious Trojan Hog, a roasted pig that when cut into spills out sausages rather than entrails. Fish also feature highly because of their sheer expense. If you have the money opt for a truly gigantic fish like a turbot, since it shows off not only that you have the coinage to buy it but also a massive kitchen to cook it in and an abundance of slaves to serve it.

Be prepared for some novelty serving of food, such as floating the dishes in water beside your couch or naked waitresses. This can also add a bit of entertaining peril to your evening, as you wait to see them spill hot sauce on themselves.

What kinds of entertainments do dinner party hosts treat their guests to?

'Treat' might be the wrong word. While munching on your Trojan Hog or killer lamprey spunk you might have the accompaniment of a poet. If you're in luck it will be a good poet. Alternatively, your host might have decided, independently of any outside corroboration, that he is an excellent poet. Or a comic. This is why it is worth enquiring ahead of time what entertainment is planned, so you can fake an illness in time.

The good host will have readings, or a singer, or perhaps a storyteller, or maybe a dancer. Be sure to clear up what kind of 'dancer', as some are known to be on the racy side.[11]

DID YOU KNOW?

The Romans would transport snow down from the mountains and serve it as a dish, sometimes flavoured with fruit juice.

What makes a bad dinner party?

Aside from the murders that often accompany an imperial dinner party, one of the most frequent complaints is a stingy host. It is not uncommon to be invited for dinner and be served lesser dishes than your host. This is a good way of signalling just where you stand in their friendship: dodgy vinegar wine versus the finest Falerian.

What do Romans drink?

Wine, of course. The best, as previously mentioned, is the Falerian variety. It gets its name from Mount Falernus, which is situated in the Italian region of Campania and on whose slopes the grapes that make Falerian wine are grown. Beware of Pompeiian wines. Though they may slip down easy enough, they are said to be responsible for the very worst hangovers.

Wine is always mixed with other ingredients, unless you want to be thought of as a complete barbarian. Water is a standard addition to wine, but also be prepared for spiced wine and honey wine. Beer is available as an alternative, but will not enhance your social standing. We advise while in Rome to do what Romans do: drink wine until you fall over.

DID YOU KNOW?

In the time of Emperor Tiberius it was considered good for your health to drink on an empty stomach.

Chapter 7

Entertainment

Will I get much leisure time?

Though the Romans have no concept of a weekend, they have compensated for this by having rather a lot of festival days and, handily, days marked as inauspicious for work. Though not, it should be pointed out, if you are a slave. The work never ends for you, I'm afraid. Rome being a thriving metropolis, it has plenty to offer in the way of distractions.

The Games

The Games are often linked to religious festivals and remain hugely popular. They are both free to attend and offer an entire day of entertainment. With that in mind be sure to bring with you:

> **A cushion** The stone seats can be very hard on the bum, particularly if you intend to attend the whole day.

> **A sun hat** There is an awning that can be pulled over the roof in hot weather, but it doesn't cover all the seats. Nobody has quite forgotten the time Caligula deliberately removed the awning at the hottest hour of the day and forbade anyone from leaving.

> **A slave** He can nip back to get anything you've forgotten to bring and get the refreshments, so you don't miss any of the day's action.

Look out for advertisements painted onto various walls in the city to ensure you don't miss out.

The place to enjoy the games is the Flavian Amphitheatre. It's dead easy to find; just look out for the 30m colossal golden statue of Nero in the nude. This statue will lend its name to what future generations call this amphitheatre.

The Flavian Amphitheatre

The Flavian Amphitheatre today.

More impressive than Egypt's pyramids, the walls of Babylon, and even the Temple at Ephesus, the Flavian Amphitheatre is the place to go. Opened in 80 CE by the current emperor's older brother, Titus, the Flavian Amphitheatre took a whopping ten years to build. The first stones were laid in 71 CE by the emperor's father, Vespasian, who sadly died before he could see his project through to completion.

It was the first stone amphitheatre in Rome and the first permanent amphitheatre too. Previously amphitheatres had been wooden in structure and put up on a temporary basis when required. It was built over the site of Nero's golden house, a controversial building since the late emperor had used land cleared by the great fire for his new palace. This led to rumours that Nero had started the great fire himself for this exact purpose (he hadn't).

Demolishing this palace was a gesture by Emperor Vespasian that he was going to give back to the people, rather than taking from them. The Jewish Wars having just been settled meant Vespasian, rather handily, had a lot of booty and a lot of slaves to build his grand edifice.

And grand it certainly is. It can hold a massive 50,000 spectators. The opening games to celebrate its completion took place over 100 days, during which 9,000 animals were slaughtered for entertainment. There were horse races and, after flooding the arena, a naval battle involving 3,000 participants.

Aside from allowing the people to enjoy such spectacles, Titus also threw down little wooden balls into the crowd. On these were inscribed prizes such as food, clothing, horses and even slaves. Whoever was lucky enough to fight off the competition for one of those wooden balls could go and collect their prize.

All of which makes it a terrible shame that after all that money, expense and effort the Flavian family put into building and exhibiting wonders at the amphitheatre, that it should be known today as the Colosseum rather than by their name.

What can I expect to see at the Games?

You can expect the very best of entertainment that Rome has to offer. First up, at the beginning of the day we have the animal shows. This is where man/woman is pitted against beast, beast is pitted against other beast, and baby elephants walk the tightrope. There really is something for everyone.

What is truly impressive is the way the arena is decorated to represent a jungle wilderness, or the plains of Africa, or even swampy marshes. Through here our heroes must traverse, while all around them await fearsome predators such as lions, hippos, crocodiles and leopards.

Generally, the audience are on the side of the beast hunters. But not always. Back in Republican days, conquering general Pompey put on an elephant hunt. Twenty of the creatures were pitted against Gaetulians[1] who were armed with spears. The elephants were having none of it and tried to break out *en masse*. When that failed, they stood in front of the audience and gave such pitiful cries that the crowd turned against Pompey and began to curse him dreadfully. Which is undoubtedly why, a few years later, Pompey lost the civil war against Caesar and was decapitated by the Egyptians.[2]

At midday we have the execution of criminals, a necessary deterrent for a city without a police force. The organisers have done their best to make this procedure entertaining by having the condemned act out scenes from mythology: there might be an Orpheus torn apart by beasts or a Prometheus having his liver pecked out.

Unless you are extremely keen on seeing Roman justice in action, you might want to skip this bit and come back for the gladiators.

In the afternoon we welcome the gladiators. Gladiators fight in pairs and come in different varieties. The most popular and most featured types in our day are:

Murmillo These are recognisable by the fish-crested helmets that they wear adorned with feathers. It's recommended that you cheer the loudest for this type of fighter as they are the emperor's favourite.

Secutor The big guys of the arena who wear a bucket-shaped helmet that completely covers their faces, except for two tiny slit holes for eyes.

Thracian Popular with the emperor's older brother, Titus, so probably safer to boo the Thracian when he comes on. Thracians fight with

Two Gladiators square up.

a rectangular shield, a spear and a sword. They have a more rounded helmet.

Retiarius Known as the net men, these gladiators fight with a net, a trident and a dagger.

What the crowd want to see from gladiators is skilled fighting and a great performance. The best gladiators dislike being paired with an inferior opponent because it gives them less chance to show off their skills.

Contrary to what you might believe, the way to win a gladiator bout is not by killing your opponent. That would quickly bankrupt the *lanista*[3] in purchasing replacements and affects repeat attendances (the crowd do like to pick a favourite to follow through their career). A sensible *lanista* carefully selects the key performance for his star gladiators so as not to overexpose them to potential injury or death, thus adding to their elusive appeal.[4]

On top of the standard gladiator show there is usually a novelty act. This might be two women fighting against each other. Or two dwarves. Or even a blind man against another visually impaired competitor. The Romans are a sucker for any type of 'novel' human. Any good emperor will try to display something or someone hitherto unseen in Rome.[5]

DID YOU KNOW?

One gladiator was so determined not to fight that he shoved the sponge on a stick that Romans used as toilet paper down his throat and choked himself.

Chariot Racing

Even more popular than the Games are the chariot races. These are held in Circus Maximus between the Aventine and Palatine Hills. Astonishingly, the Circus can hold a crowd of 250,000 spectators, a quarter of Rome's total population.

Chariots are attached to four horses and raced around the 600m track. There is no real reason why four horses are used rather than two, it is not any faster but there is an increased chance of crashes, or shipwrecks as the Romans call them, which adds to the entertainment.

Competitors race in teams: the Blues, the Greens, the Whites and the Reds.[6] All come with their own fanatical followers who are quite prepared to use magic to curse the opposing chariot teams.

Gambling is a major part of the races which perhaps explains some of these extreme reactions from the fans. The races are fast, furious, extremely dangerous but thrilling. Which explains their continuing popularity.

DID YOU KNOW?

One fan of the Reds racing team was so distraught at the death of his hero driver that he threw himself onto the charioteer's funeral pyre.

The Charioteering Emperor

The Emperor Nero was absolutely fanatical about chariot racing. As a teenager he had a mini chariot set made out of ivory that he used to play with when he should have been doing emperor-type things.

As he got older Nero realised that being emperor meant he didn't have to do emperor-type things; he could race chariots instead. This being sort of thing the senators sneered at, his advisors set him up with a secret racetrack in the Vatican valley so that nobody would know about it. But what was the fun of racing if there are no crowds?

Keen to placate him, an audience of slaves and other lower-class persons was assembled in the Circus Maximus for the emperor to race in front of. Naturally, rather than sating his obsession, it only increased it. Nero set off to Greece to source a bigger audience. He toured the province taking part in the Panhellenic Games.[7]

It was at the Olympic Games that the emperor took on his most daring challenge to date: driving a ten-horse chariot round the track.

Could he do it? Would he win the Olympic crown? No, he couldn't and yes, he did. Nero crashed his chariot fairly spectacularly, but the Olympians thought it politic to declare him the winner anyhow. He returned to Rome much in the manner of a triumphant general, having won 1,808 prizes in total during his two-year tour.

Theatre

This is very much a lower-class pastime and that is reflected in the type of plays performed. Expect bawdy tales of cunning slaves, long-lost siblings, pirates and, in the case of one play, farting clowns. The actors wear masks to depict their characters' expressions.

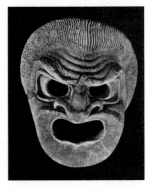

Like chariot teams, actors attract fanatical followers. Under the Emperor Tiberius things got out of hand when both actors and fans were kicked out of Rome after expressions of their devotion descended into a public brawl.

Theatre mask.

Gambling

Gambling takes place in the cookshops and taverns, but also on the street. Gaming tables are scratched into the pavements all over Rome. The most popular games involve dice rolling with huge stakes placed on the result. The Emperor Claudius was so fanatical about dicing that he wrote a book on the subject and had a board fitted to his carriage so he could play while travelling. Nero would stake 4,000 gold pieces on a single roll of the dice.

Cheats abound, so we'd recommend you stay clear of staking your posh new fur-lined cloak and fancy sandals. The law does state that debtors can be physically torn apart by their creditors as a form of execution. There are no examples of this overly severe punishment actually being carried out, but it's always best to err on the side of caution. It's distinctly less painful.

The Baths

Bathing in ancient Rome is not a private activity, it's a very public one, and one which everyone from the rich to the poor partake in. Rome has many public baths including a very impressive one built by Nero. As Martial puts it: 'What is worse than Nero? What is better than Nero's baths?'[8]

The bathhouse is the place to socialise, choose a book from the library, acquire dinner party invitations, get your armpits plucked, take a walk in the gardens, work out in the gym and maybe have a bit of a wash.

Where can I find a bathhouse?

There are three imperially built bath complexes that are worth a visit. Those magnificent baths of Nero are situated on the Campus Martius near to the baths of Agrippa (Augustus' son-in-law and right-hand guy). The baths of Titus are handily situated next to the Flavian Amphitheatre, so you can get the sweat scraped off your face after a particularly tense gladiator match. The baths of Titus are worth a nose around, since they were constructed from bits of Nero's golden house, so now's your chance to see what all the fuss was about.

What should I expect when I go to the baths?

There are three different bathing experiences: the cold bath *frigidarium*, the warm bath *tepidarium* and the hot bath *caldarium*. One should move from one temperature to the next to gain the full experience. A slave will rub oil into your skin and then scrape it off along with all the dirt with a tool called a *strigil*, after which you might have a massage or head for the main pool to catch up on all the gossip.

DID YOU KNOW?

Not only did the Romans bathe in public fully naked, they also had mixed bathing sessions which both men and women could attend.

As well as being social, relaxing and a good way to kill a few hours, bathing has health benefits. It relieves fatigue, cures headaches and aids a recovery from pneumonia. Though doctors strongly advise avoidance of the baths should you be suffering from a looseness of your bowels, for everyone else's sake as well as your own. However, the modern visitor to the baths might well question whether there are truly any health benefits when the water is rarely changed.

Anything I need to be aware of when going to the baths?

Put a slave to guarding your clothes or tip one of the bath slaves to do so. Thieves are everywhere.

Romans haven't quite decided whether the baths are a suitable, relaxing way to spend time or whether they are effeminising dens of depravity. It would be foolish to pretend that dodgier elements aren't motivated by the naked attractions of the baths, though this could work in your favour. Certain notable patrons have been known to dish out those all-important dinner party invites at the baths based purely on what their eye has fallen on. If such attentions bother you be sure to take a slave to accompany you, or, if you can't afford a slave, a burly friend.

Chapter 8

Health and medicine

What diseases would I be most vulnerable to?

The Romans have a very different understanding of diseases. They believe that if you fall ill this is due to an imbalance in your humours. There are four of these humours:

- Blood – which is warm and moist.
- Yellow Bile – which is warm and dry.
- Black Bile – which is cold and dry.
- Phlegm – which is cold and moist.

Depending on your age and gender, you will be more susceptible to an imbalance of a certain humour that will need to be corrected. Children are considered warm and moist. Young men are warm and dry. Mature men are cold and dry. Old men are cold and moist. Women are notably moister than men, which is why it is important that they menstruate, otherwise their system would be overwhelmed with excess fluid and cause ill health.

You can expect an excess of phlegm in wintertime due to the cold and damp, similarly in summer expect your yellow bile to go nuts. The location of these imbalances determines your illness; for example, a build-up of black bile in your brain is responsible for melancholy, while a mass of yellow bile in that organ causes delirium.

Despite their adherence to the humours health model, the Romans have not ignored the fact that if you live by a swampy area you have a tendency to pick up a strange, deadly fever, though they believe this to be due to the air, rather than mosquitos. Plagues similarly confuse them since they afflict all genders and ages indiscriminately. They have squared this non-humour fitting peg by declaring plagues to be the work of very angry gods.

Realistically, in a very crowded city with no vaccines or antibiotics, nor any understanding of sterilisation, you are likely to get sick quite a lot. This is particularly true if you are a child: mortality of the under fives is high. Also, childbirth is extremely dangerous and any complication in labour is likely to be fatal. Caesareans are performed, but at the expense of the mother's life as she will not survive the operation.

DID YOU KNOW?

Julius Caesar, contrary to the stories, was not born by caesarean section. His mother Aurelia lived to a ripe old age.

This may sound all very dispiriting, but really there has never been a better time in antiquity for the treatment of certain injuries. Should you happen to be shot with an arrow by a disgruntled neighbour (possibly because of that cockerel alarm of yours) or get slingshot pellets in your bum from an enraged creditor, Rome is the place to live. Experience with battlefield casualties means there is expertise in removing even the most stubborn projectile from you most delicate areas. And the good news is you're likely to survive.

Imperial illnesses

Though all the empire offers up daily prayers to the gods that the emperor might forever enjoy good health, this is not always enough. Emperors can and do fall ill. Here are some examples.

Augustus
The first of Rome's emperors may have lived well into his seventies but he frequently suffered from ill health. Some of this happened to coincide with major battles in which he was due to fight, which I am sure we can all agree was just unfortunate timing. Amongst his ailments was ringworm, a tightness of breath at certain times of

---

the year[1] and a weakness in the forefinger of his right hand which severely impaired his ability to point at things.

Tiberius

Though Rome's second emperor followed the health fad of the day, drinking on an empty stomach, this did not save him from embarrassing teenage acne and then, in his older age, a skin condition so embarrassing that he ran away to Capri and never showed his (scabby) face again in Rome.

Caligula

Caligula was a sick one, both in body and mind. In his youth he suffered from epilepsy and regularly found himself unable to walk due to faintness. During the early part of his reign he fell dangerously ill and was not expected to live. The kind citizen who offered up his own life to the gods if they would spare the young emperor came to regret this pledge when a newly recovered Caligula demanded he fulfil this promise. The somewhat unstable emperor was also afflicted with insomnia and rarely slept more than three hours a night, which might explain a lot.

Claudius

Where to start with Claudius? He was born with a set of afflictions that had his own mother declaring him a monster. He stammered, his head shook, he would foam at the mouth and his nose would trickle. However, these traits only seemed to appear at moments of high emotion when he was emperor.[2] It seems that he may have exaggerated his symptoms when younger as a survival mechanism in the vipers' nest that was the Julio Claudian family. It was evidently a successful strategy.

Nero

Disgustingly healthy despite the endless banquets and dissipation, which makes those of us with delicate stomachs quite jealous.

Galba

In his seventies when he became emperor, Galba suffered from crippling gout and wore a corset to deal with his back issues. Neither of which affected his hobby of collecting sturdy young men.

Is there anything I can do to prevent illnesses?

Obviously, diseases spread easier in overcrowded spaces so you might consider leaving Rome for the countryside. Avoid the swampy countryside because that's where malaria lurks. Also, towns that are western facing and get the sun from early morning are thus more likely to tilt your humours towards the dry and hot scale. In fact, it's worth checking out what the wind direction of your chosen fleeing spot is, as this also affects the balance of your humours (cold winds a quarter between north west and north east, for example, are going to give you terrible constipation.)

If you can't face voluntary exile from the greatest city on earth (and are too confused by the effect of wind directions on your bowels to make a reasoned decision) you might want to consider magic. Romans have numerous incarnations that are thought to prevent you from harm. For example, should you happen to come across a scorpion, saying the word 'two' will stop it from stinging you. Before making a journey, you should always repeat a prayer three times to ensure you make it to the end in the one piece. We can add to the Vestal Virgins' catalogue of privileges the ability to freeze runaway slaves to the spot with a spoken spell.[3] Spells are also available to spot bleeding, cure sciatica and do wonders for your gout.

You might also want to invest in a protective amulet. Children wear the protective *bulla* or *luna* amulets round their necks, but a range of such amulets are also available for adults. The luckiest, most protecting and most versatile amulets are phallus shaped. You will see these everywhere, from the shopkeeper hanging an erect member outside his door in the hope of a thriving business, to the spectator scrawling one in the masonry of the Flavian amphitheatre to help his favourite gladiator. See also phallus rings, charms and wind chimes. We'd recommend acclimatising yourself to the sight of phalluses prior to your visit, lest you embarrass yourself with a giggle.[4]

Other ways to protect yourself from illness are rather boring and mundane in comparison to penis jewellery: sleep well, eat well, exercise and don't overindulge. Sexual overindulgence is extremely bad for your health, sometimes even fatal. Abstinence on the other hand is to be admired as good old-fashioned Roman fortitude, although only after you've produced the required three children.

Lucky hanging phallus with bells on.

What should I do if I do fall ill?

You could put your trust in the gods. True, they haven't worked very hard at preventing your illness, but that's most likely down to you and your paltry offerings. Consider it a lesson in respecting and venerating ALL gods and not just the ones you think will help you get off with that sexy barmaid/gladiator.

If sacrificing at your local temple doesn't seem to be helping your ailment, there is always the option of travelling to a bigger, better temple with a proven track record in cures. The temple of Asclepius in Epidaurus, Greece, is rightly famous for curing the diseased and sick. Testaments abound of the miraculous effects of visiting this temple: kidney stones have vanished; infertile women have got up the duff; a small boy with a hideous growth had it licked by a temple dog and the growth was gone; that bald bloke who was fed up with being mocked got a hairy head.

DID YOU KNOW?

The temple of Asclepius in Rome was built in 290 BCE on an island in the Tiber river after a terrible plague hit the city.

If you don't fancy having your ailment licked away by a dog, you could always visit a hot spring. These are renowned for their healing abilities and also make you smell a lot nicer.

If you can't travel, or if none of the above works, it might be time to seek the help of a doctor. Doctors come in two varieties: the useless and the dangerous.[5] But if the gods have abandoned you, then you really have nothing to lose by seeking one out.

What to look for in a doctor

There are no formal qualifications or set training to become a doctor in ancient Rome. Anyone can call themselves a doctor, which is why you need to be on your guard for quacks and charlatans who will happily con you out of much-needed coinage with fake cures and ludicrous advice.

This is why many prefer to rely on the gods, who, though they may be mysterious and unfathomable, don't boss you about and then charge you for the privilege.

When seeking a doctor, do quiz them thoroughly on their background. The best doctors are always Greek,[6] though a great number of Romans are bilingual in Latin and Greek, so throwing a series of Greek phrases is unlikely in itself to uncover a fake. However, it is easy enough to bombard them with questions about their stated city of birth, which will help you sort your Athens-born from your down the road Aventine-hill born.

Many doctors do not work full time and often have second jobs. You should immediately discount these people, since it shows they are not successful enough to practise full time. Unless their second job has a clearly transferable skill, such as a barber or butcher, who will at least be trained in the use of a sharp instrument for lobbing off that gangrenous foot of yours.

Be wary of public demonstrations by doctors. Although it may be an entertaining spectacle, it may not be all it seems and there is likely to be a bit of staging and acting going on. Reputable doctors do not see medicine as an entertainment for the crowd to gawp at.

Your best bet in finding a good doctor is to ask for recommendations from your healthy friends. A good doctor should, naturally, be astonishingly well himself. Look out for signs of dissipation; many doctors are known for their overindulgence in both wine and women.

DID YOU KNOW?

Augustus was so pleased with his Greek doctor, Antonius Musa, that he had a statue sculpted of him and placed it next to the healing god, Asclepius.

What to expect from a trip to the doctors

You should expect lots and lots of questions, such as the content of your dreams,[8] the exact spot where you live,[9] your diet, your life history and the consistency of your poos. He will also probably stare at you for a long time;

this is called an 'observation'[10] and from this 'observation' he will make recommendations on how to relieve yourself of those tiresome symptoms.

DID YOU KNOW?

Animal dung is a proven remedy for many complaints. Sheep dung is good for pimples, mouse dung for baldness, dog dung for tonsillitis and stork dung for seizures.

If I fall ill, what treatment will my doctor prescribe?

Breathe easy, it's not at all horrible. Most treatments advised by Roman doctors veer towards the pleasant side: cutting out the booze, massage, outings in the fresh air and a nice hot bath (or cold bath if suffering from a fever).

He might suggest regular exercise, reading aloud to practise a proper breathing regime, or a trip to the seaside with a ride on a boat so that your internal organs might benefit from the gentle rocking motion. He might even suggest sexual intercourse as a remedy for many maladies, including depression, back pain, weakened eyesight, blocked up nose and a snake bite. But, as noted previously, be wary of having too much sex. Balance is everything.

You will have your fair share of horrible cures, however, so brace yourself for these. Sore gums may be helped by a thorough scraping with the tooth of a man who has met a violent end. It doesn't say whether you should be the cause of that violent end for the treatment to be effective, so we'd recommend you avoid embroiling yourself in murder. On a similar theme, rabies is cured by swallowing the ground-down skull of a hanged man. Should you be suffering from a decline in sexual oomph, the sweat of a gladiator is a well-known aphrodisiac and will sort out your love life in no time.

Also on the unpleasant side, much of Roman medicine involves purging oneself; that is, being made to vomit repeatedly. Leeches and other methods of bloodletting are also commonly used. Women can expect to have incense puffed up their vaginas to ascertain their fertility, cupping-glasses to be suckered to their nipples to stop menstruation, or to have hemlock rubbed on their breasts to firm them up.

Eating your way to health

The first aspect all doctors will concern themselves with is diet. Pliny the Elder has a lengthy list of foods that are good for particular ailments.

Cucumbers – Are great for both poor eyesight and styes. Additionally, dried cucumber roots work for scabies and ringworm.

Onions – Good for the bowels and can be used as a suppository for haemorrhoids.[11]

Lettuce – An indispensable part of your larder, lettuce disperses flatulence and suppresses burps, which can only be good for your social standing.

Cabbage – Good for headaches and spots before the eyes. Pounded cabbage can be applied to fistulas and sprains. Also, if eaten before drinking it will stop intoxication (which makes you wonder what the point of the drinking is).

Vinegar – Good for coughs, asthma, shrinkage of the gums. Also cited as an antidote to asp bites.

Walnuts – Helps expel tapeworms. Old walnuts can cure gangrene and bruises. Excitingly, if you eat two dried walnuts, two figs, and twenty leaves of rue with a pinch of salt you are immune to poison that whole day. Provided you take it on an empty stomach.

Acorns – Boiled, they aid dysentery.

Juniper – Good for toothache.

Moss – Add to a bath to ease infections of lady parts.

Crushed holly leaves – Good for diseases of the joints.

What about pain relief if I get sick? Is there anything I can take to relieve it?

You could take Stoic philosopher Seneca's advice and just suck it up. He recommended that a friend who was suffering agonising pain should use boxers and wrestlers as role models, given how they suffer pain for fame in silence. He also consoles the friend that if the pain is really that severe, then the illness will be a swift one and the pain will soon end: because he'll be dead. All of which proves that Seneca has a lousy bedside manner and should definitely not be called upon for sympathy when you've got a miserable cold, or, indeed, are writhing around in agony.

The most familiar of these pain-relieving drugs are poppies, aka opium, which is also recommended as an aid to sleep.[12] Also suggested for pain relief are juniper (excellent for killing toothache apparently) and mandrake, the smell of which knocks people unconscious.

However, should you be in need of surgery there are no anaesthetics available. This poses an ethical dilemma to the surgeon: should he work quickly and end your torment all the sooner, or should he take his time to be precise, which might make the surgery more successful but your suffering agonies all the much longer? Either way, to be a surgeon one needs a certain distance of mind and an unflappable nature. As for the patient, they are recommended to be fettered to the table and have their ears blocked with wool. Apparently hearing the sound of your bones being chipped away has been proven to upset some patients. Who'd have thought it?

Graeco-Roman surgical instruments.

Chapter 9

Work

What kinds of jobs are available in Ancient Rome?

There are many jobs available, but there is a problem. In the job market you will be competing against those offering free labour, namely slaves. It is of particular worry to Romans that slaves are dominating the job market. Any big campaign or war will flood the city with new captives and their labour, which is bad news for local labourers. However, there are still plenty of jobs available in a city the size of Rome for the enterprising incomer. We've identified a few that you might want to try out.

Being Nero

The account of the Emperor Nero's death is so very detailed[1] that it clearly had to come from one of the three people present at the time: his two freedmen, Epaphroditus and Phaon, plus his favourite eunuch, Sporus. This has not stopped many refusing to believe that Nero is dead. Possibly because every few years someone pops up claiming to be him. Pretending to be Nero could be a suitable job for you.

To date, there have been three men claiming to be the sadly missed emperor. The first appeared only a year after Nero's actual death. The second popped up in Asia, when Titus was emperor. Then five years ago, the Parthians were wild with joy when they discovered they had a Caesar amongst them. So joyful that they decided to raise an army to help the poor befallen emperor back on his throne.[2]

There are clear benefits in pretending to be Nero. The key one being that everybody will love you. No really, they will. You may have heard that Nero was a terrible emperor who everybody hated, but that is a

LIE. Clearly shown by the popularity of the three fake Neros, who were cheerfully accepted.

Indeed, being Nero can enable you to attract your own army. Obviously, there are various benefits to having your own army beyond basking in their love of you/Nero. Having your own army means you can get things you want, such as movable objects, women or territory.

You also don't need much in the way of training or skills to be Nero. A slight physical resemblance helps. As does some ability in playing the lyre and singing. But don't panic if you lack pitch, for nobody is quite sure whether Nero was any good or whether he won all those prizes because he was the emperor and had an army.

The downside to being Nero is that it is unlikely to hold long-term career prospects. Either your newly formed army will discover you're not Nero and be peeved or the actual emperor will get peeved at you for causing trouble all over his provinces. Peevishness of this level will lead to your death.

But for a brief glorious moment you will have the adoration and loyalty of the many, which some would consider worth an ignoble end. But really the decision is yours.

Court Poet

Though the emperor favours his staff for all the best jobs (naturally), there are a few openings at the palace for an outsider. If you are good with words, then poetry might be a calling for you. Be warned, though, this field is highly competitive and you must use all of your contacts to find a way in. Your best bet is to make friends with a palace freedman, like myself. Being close to the emperor, we are in a good position to place your poems in the imperial library, or even to put them before the emperor himself.[3]

We do get many such requests, so might I suggest you win favour by some small gift. Money is always welcome. Or perhaps you might write a poem all about me, as a taster for what the emperor might expect. Nobody wants to inflict bad poetry on the emperor, or indeed his staff.

The work of a court poet can be summed up in one word: flattery. It is your job to flatter the emperor and make him feel good about himself and all that he has achieved. Thankfully, his Imperial Majesty Emperor Domitian has ruled for fifteen years, which means there is quite a lot of stuff he's done that is worthy of a poem.

Subjects other court poets have written about include:

- The emperor's campaigns in Germania (which you must insist were a marvellous success);
- The emperor's fabulous new palace: 'The gods rejoice to see you installed in a palace equalling their own';[4]
- The road the emperor built (which has really improved journey times to the coast);
- When the emperor widened the streets (and it was really handy and made getting places better);
- The emperor's anti-castration laws (which have made all men feel much more secure about their bits);
- How marvellous the emperor's staff are (which is so very true);
- The emperor's favourite eunuch, Earinus (who is the undeserved subject of several poems);
- The time the emperor went away and then came back again (and we were all glad about it);
- That time the emperor was at the games and it snowed, and the snow fell on the emperor's face (no mention of the imperial staff having wet, cold feet and trembling limbs, mind);
- Earinus again (grrr).

The emperor's house, better than the pyramids by far.

As someone very close to our dear Imperial Majesty, I can advise that the emperor does enjoy a nice line on how wonderful he is. Such as this one from Martial: 'No ruler, Caesar, has Rome ever so loved before, and she could not love you more, even were she to desire it.'[5]

He also rather enjoys being compared to Jupiter. A top tip is to try using Jupiter's other name, Jove, as it is far easier to find words to rhyme with it.

NB There are some subjects best avoided so as to not upset the emperor, such as his baldness, his bandy legs and that time his wife had a fling with that actor.

Being an Oddity

In a crowded world you need to use whatever attributes you possess to stand out. If you happen to own any physical deformities/oddities now is the time to whip them out. Literally. Because the Romans adore a bit of weirdness. The weirder your attribute, the higher your chance of monetary reward. At the absolute high end you might attract the eye of the emperor and gain a place at court.

We are told that the great Emperor Augustus used to display anything strange/remarkable to entertain the public. You could be that entertainment.

What do you need to succeed at being an oddity? The short answer is something worth showing. This is not as easy as you might think. Many Romans have served and been injured in the legions, so missing limbs, noses and brutal scars are very, very common.

DID YOU KNOW?

Soldier Marcus Sergius didn't let the small matter of having his right hand severed stop him taking part in battles. He had an artificial iron one fitted.

Also, this is a city where parents happily name their children 'warty lambkin',[6] so it needs to be something good. Useful attributes to sell are excessive height, although you'll be competing with the ten-foot-tall Gabbara from Arabia who toured Rome under the Emperor Claudius. Excessive shortness, or dwarfism, is particularly valued, though watch out you don't end up in the arena in a 'comedy' fight section against the blind or a woman.

Excessive size of some part of you plays well. Emperor Domitian is very fond of a small boy who has an extremely large head. So fond, in fact, that he is known to take political advice from him. Just think, that freakishly large big toe you have could propel you all the way to handing out advice to the emperor.

Legacy Hunter

This is the perfect job for those possessed of charm but lacking in ethics. The legacy hunter secures an income by convincing the more mature Roman to write them into their will and leave them a heap of money.

The way to do this is by becoming extremely dear to them. Be warned this is very time consuming. You need to be constantly in their thoughts, which means you need to be constantly with them. Pop up at breakfast to enquire whether they had pleasant dreams, hang around being 'company' until midday, attend every one of their dinner parties, even if you don't fancy it. The role of a legacy hunter is hard work.

You might also want to surprise your target with special acts of thoughtfulness, such as hiring your own physicians to tend to their ailments. Or bringing in an astrologer to console them that their illness will soon pass. Organise expensive sacrifices to the gods for your dearest friend's good health and tell them the exact number of oxen dispatched, so they may know of your thoughtfulness and how much money it cost you.

If you're short of coinage, don't worry, there are other, cheaper methods of securing a legacy. On being asked to witness the will of a wealthy lady, one keen legacy hunter saw an immediate opportunity. He insisted the lady leave him some money, standing over her until she did so.[7] Though menacing your way to a fortune only works if you can prevent another less favourable will being written the minute you leave the room.

Alternatively, you could rely on your other 'charms' (nudge, nudge, wink, wink). There is an opportunity in, let us say, courting the rich and lonely.

As a job, legacy hunting has the potential to make you very, very rich. However, the downside is that people will hate you, which you may decide you can weather given a massive house and a well-stacked wine cellar.

DID YOU KNOW?

Being adopted as an adult was common amongst the upper classes in Rome. The wealthy and childless would often adopt an adult male to continue their family name.

If all other employment options fail, you can always join the army. There may be downsides (a horrible, mangled death being just one) but it is secure employment for twenty-five years. A true job for life.

Do women work? What types of jobs do they do?

Contrary to how our current Imperial Morality Master would like it, women can and do work. Not me, obviously. I am far too busy to work, though being social in this town is hard enough work on its own. It takes a lot of labour to be this charming, I tell you!

But other women do. Here are some of the employment opportunities for women in ancient Rome:

Midwife

What could be more important than bringing the next generation of Romans into the world? A midwife needs to be of good character, be literate, be sympathetic, have nice short nails (of course) and soft hands.

The latter excuses you from any activity that might harden those hands, such as weaving and wool working, and anything else you don't fancy doing. The downside is that you are expected to remain sober at all times – which is no fun – lest you receive a call out. This is also the case with a lot of labouring women. Personally, during my first (horrendous) labour I could cheerfully have punched my sober, sympathetic midwife. Though she did have lovely, manicured nails.

Wet Nurse

The world of work is all about making the best of what you have. We ladies have two assets that the men don't: breasts. Wet nurses are the baby equivalent of a delicious takeaway delivered straight to your door. They appear on your doorstep and take those screaming red-faced creatures away, giving you the chance for a well-earned nap. They are an absolute marvel, highly skilled and seeping milk into their tunics at every hour of the day and night, ready to service.

A wet nurse is a very suitable career for those who like babies and like sitting down for hours with one attached to their nipple. Be warned, though, that any good employer will wish to check your credentials before appointing. They will be looking for a good-sized breast and nipple, so be prepared to whip them out. Though maybe wait until asked, in order to avoid a dreadfully awkward situation.

Money Lender

To keep up with the latest fashion costs coinage, and annoyingly coinage is not always available. Particularly when you've been afflicted with a useless husband, as I so often have.

When I face a simply gorgeous silver curtained litter and an empty purse, I turn to my friend Delia. She has a sideline lending her husband's money out, with interest payable naturally. She tells me it is a marvellous job since she gets to see inside all the best houses and is first up with the gossip as to who has purchased a matching pair of Ethiopian eunuchs this month. The only downside, she says, about the moneylending business is when people don't pay up what they owe. Then she's forced to send round five of her hardest slaves to duff them up and seize goods to the value of the debt. Though she says she really doesn't like doing this.

Poisoner

This is a more specialist role, but one frequently in demand at the palace. How else do you think they sort out those tricky succession issues? Poison is very much a lady's weapon of choice. Not me. I prefer those metal knuckle dusters that boxers wear, but each to their own.

The most famous lady poisoner of all time is Locusta, a dear old lady who bumped off both Emperor Claudius and his son, Britannicus, to clear the way for Nero's reign. For this she was rewarded with a lovely country estate. Poisoning then, can be lucrative, but do think carefully on your stance regarding the ethics of murder before you dive into employment.

Sorceress

Mixing together herbs and plants in order to murder someone might be a bit too far for us squeamish sorts, but what about mixing together herbs and plants in order to inflict impotence? That sounds far more appealing and is one of the many skills of the sorceress.

Potions are not the only weapon in the sorceress' arsenal. There are also spells, charms and little wax figures that you can satisfyingly stab with pins. Not that I've ever done that. Much.

Sorceresses are the go-to woman for all manner of problems you need solving, but their particular speciality is in the realm of love. Suffering awfully from unrequited love? Go see your local sorceress for a love potion to make him fall passionately in love with you. Worried that your lover's wife will find out about your wild affair? The sorceress can help you there too, by casting an ignorance spell. Top tip: these spells are also handy when you don't want your husband to get annoyingly huffy over those trifling debts you might have accumulated. Then, when the love affair goes terribly wrong (as they so often do, because, well, men) and the scummy bum sponge takes up with some other lady, your local sorceress can provide just the tonic needed: a willy-limping potion!

Other services offered by a sorceress include interpreting dreams, which sounds dreadful. Can you imagine anything duller than listening to other people's tedious dreams? But apparently it pays, and there is always the opportunity to charge extra for exorcising those bad dreams away. I should warn you, though, that occasionally the emperor gets a bit fed up with sorceresses and decides it would be a terrific idea if you all left Rome. I would advise investing in a nice seaside villa in case of such an eventuality, where you can wait it out in comfort.

Chapter 10

Warfare

Rome, of course, is famous for her army. Without the army there would be no empire, no roads, none of that expensive perfume from Arabia that you love, and a severe shortage of slaves to nip down the shops for you.

Who can join the army?

Pretty much anyone in the empire can join the army. With a few restrictions, naturally. As with every part of Roman life, women and non-citizens are not wanted. But if you are male, hold your citizenship and can sport a full set of limbs and digits, you are in. Provided you don't have a wife; soldiers are officially banned from getting married. Unofficially they may accidentally make some kind of commitment to a lady that is definitely not marriage but may involve children of varying sizes acquired over many years.

What are the benefits of enlisting in the army?

The benefits are many. The pay isn't bad at 1200 sesterces a year. Though do bear in mind you will be expected to pay for your own equipment and clothing out of that. There is the opportunity to be posted anywhere, from the chilly climate of wild Britannia, to the sunny sands of Egypt. Travel broadens the mind, they say, and travelling in the Roman army will broaden your mind enough to recognise that Rome is greatest place on the planet, and everywhere else is inhabited by barbarians intent on killing you. Then there's the camaraderie that only comes with having to share a small leather tent for years at a time, while surrounded by a resentful local population who hate all Romans. Also, at the end of your service you will receive a small plot of land.

Roman legionary and centurion. Note the centurion's whacking stick.

What are the downsides of enlisting in the army?

It is quite a commitment. Once enlisted you will serve twenty-five years. Dependent, of course, on not falling victim to a random accident during training, a not so random accident from an enemy soldier, or a punch up over whose helmet is the shiniest.

It's probably worth mentioning that there will be a fair amount of marching. In fact, a lot of marching. Therefore, before you enlist you might want to weigh up your feelings on marching, because it's what you'll be doing every single day, sometimes several times a day, for twenty-five years. On the positive side a Roman army on the march is quite a sight to behold and there's a definite kick from stomping in formation through the provinces for those who enjoy being menacing on a large scale. Just make sure you invest in a comfy pair of sandals.

Being defeated

The Roman army may be the best in the world, but that doesn't mean it is entirely unbeaten in combat. They have, on rare occasions, tasted the bitterly awful taste of defeat. Because these events are so infrequent, they occupy a particular part of the Roman psyche, one of great shame and humiliation that beats down centuries later. It pains us, therefore, to record the greatest of these Roman army kickings, but here they are:

The Killing Fields: Battle of Cannae, August 216 BCE

The battle of Cannae took place during the second Punic war against the Carthaginians (the one with the elephants). One August day, 86,000 Roman troops faced up to Hannibal's lesser army of 40,000.[1] It looked like it would be a casual stroll of a victory, but Hannibal had a cunning plan.

Facing off against the Roman foe, he steadily and slowly grew the length of his troop line. Then he ordered them to move inwards, forming a crescent shape that enveloped and surrounded the Roman forces. It was a bloody massacre of epic proportions, with the Romans helplessly surrounded and fighting in all directions as the Carthaginians methodically picked them off. One historian claims 600 legionaries were slaughtered every minute.[2]

Disaster in the Desert: Battle of Carrhae, 53 BCE

Rome had been doing very well in the East, sucking up Syria, Judaea and large chunks of Asia Minor.[3] Roman General, Marcus Licinius Crassus, saw no reason why Parthia[4] shouldn't be added to this growing Roman domain. In 53 BCE he marched seven legions into Parthian territory, convinced of victory.

This arrogance was the key to the disaster. Crassus and his legions marched into the desert knowing absolutely nothing about the Parthians, their forces or their fighting tactics. They assumed Rome would be victorious and had no clue as to the horrors they were about to face.

The Parthians, unbeknown to the Romans, had a very particular talent: they were expert horsemen and archers. They could fire their armour-piercing arrows at the invading Romans from a safe distance away. Also a safe distance away were the camels loaded up with spare arrows. So there really was no end to the Romans' torture.[5]

Crassus and most of his 30,000 strong legionaries were slaughtered. This victory cheered the Parthians so much they thought they'd invade Syria while they were on a roll. They were very narrowly held back by one of Crassus' few surviving commanders, Cassius.[6]

Meanwhile, somewhere deep in Parthian territory, a play was being staged for the delight of the king. However, they were missing a very important prop for *The Bacchae*. Handily, Crassus' decapitated head was hanging about backstage, so they used that.[7]

Varus, Varus, Give Me Back my Legions: The Teutoburg Forest, 9 CE

Governor of Germania, Varus, made the boob of his career when trusting the word of supposedly Romanised[8] German prince, Arminius. Arminius led Varus and his three legions into an ambush by local tribes. All of Varus's forces, some 20,000 men, were slaughtered. So upset was he by this disaster, the Emperor Augustus was said to wander about the palace crying, 'Varus, Varus, give me back my legions!'

How much fighting will I do?

That is really dependent on where you find yourself posted. You are unlikely to find much combat in sunny North Africa, for instance. However, find yourself posted on the Rhine border in Germania and you are likely to find most of your time is spent skirmishing with the more aggressive German tribes.

The present emperor, Domitian, is keen on building his own military reputation, meaning there is a high chance you might face a battle. In recent years the emperor has personally led an army against the notoriously prickly German tribe, the Chatti. He has also pursued campaigns against the Dacians[9] and very nearly brought the wild Caledonians into the empire.[10]

DID YOU KNOW?

The Emperor Domitian's campaign against the Chatti failed to capture enough enemy soldiers for his triumph, so a group of slaves were dressed up as Chatti tribesmen instead.

On the upside, if you manage not to be killed during a campaign, you might get to take part in the triumph. This is a truly spectacular event where the victorious general/emperor rides before his triumphant army through the streets of Rome to cheering crowds. Accompanying the jubilant legionaries are all the bits they've nicked from the conquered province, such as treasures and enemy soldiers.

DID YOU KNOW?

As well as marching twenty-five miles a day, Roman legionaries have to carry their equipment on their back.

How do Romans fight?

Up close and personal, which is why you are issued with a shield to hide behind. The Roman army is so successful partly due to its sheer size, but also down to its organisation. Romans are very organised, and they do love a great to-do list. A general Roman to-do list will include: march, build camp, kill enemy, steal enemy's treasures and enslave them, march.

More particularly, every soldier will know what their role is within the legion. This could be as one of the initial scouts sent on ahead to check out the enemy positions and report back; or as one of the engineers who will travel ahead of the main legion and ensure the roads are fit for marching on and that there are bridges across any inconveniently placed rivers; or perhaps you are a Centurion charged with being really quite shouty at recruits.

Whichever you are, you will know where you need to be and what you need to do when the enemy advances. This is because you will have taken part in ludicrously long and hard drills re-enacting this very scenario. If, for any reason, you suddenly forget absolutely everything you've been taught as a soldier, there's always a shouty centurion on hand to bellow instructions right in your ear.

DID YOU KNOW?

The Roman general, Corbulo, in trying to whip his army into shape insisted they sleep under canvas tents despite the harsh weather. Many men lost limbs to frostbite and some even died on guard duty.

Romans fight in formation, which means every man gets the benefit from his neighbour's shield. Advancing in a tight line means you can use those shields to push into the enemy' ranks and then use the long, pointed dagger you've been issued with to stab your way to victory.

Backing up the front-line legionary, the Roman army has some serious firepower. First up we have the archers, who will fill the sky with arrows and hopefully bump off enough of the enemy in advance of the front line engaging them. For added deadly force, the archers will set fire to their arrows before pinging them at the enemy.

Romans are highly suspicious of archery. As it doesn't involve physical contact there is a concern that it's not terribly manly. Yes, every elite Roman boy will have a go at firing off some arrows, but as a hobby or for hunting, not in warfare.[11] Therefore, the ever-practical Romans have outsourced this skill and employ mainly Syrians as their archers.[12]

Elsewhere we find the slingers. These are armed with a length of leather which they will swing round their heads at great speed, releasing sharpened stones or lead at the enemy. To make these even more wounding, it is common practise to carve insults on these projectiles. During a falling out with Mark Antony's wife, Fulvia, Augustus fired stones inscribed with some rather less than favourable sentiments about the part of Fulvia's anatomy they were aiming for.[13]

Reconstruction of a ballista.

The Romans also have access to some more serious, bigger, bulkier firepower: artillery. The ballista, which resembles a massive cross bow, shoots huge bolts at the enemy by way of springs made from animal bits and hair. Massive stones are flung in the air by attacking Romans using a catapult. Catapults are either propelled by use of weights or by being wound back and then released (using the same type of springs as used on the ballista).

Artillery comes in most useful when besieging a town, something the Romans have truly perfected. They even have specialist siege equipment: battering rams, towers and, the more mundane but definitely useful, ladders. Tunnelling under the city walls is another favourite tactic, as is building a mound the same height as the walls to allow the perfect deployment of your legionaries.

Famous sieges include the siege of Carthage,[14] which lasted three whole years, the siege of Masada, whose clifftop location was repelled by the Romans building a huge ramp they could pull their artillery up,[15] and the siege of Veii,[16] when the Romans successfully tunnelled under the walls and surprised the inhabitants.

But before we completely marvel over how truly superior the Romans were at siege warfare, let us mention the siege of Placentia.

This took place during the civil wars of 69 CE. The northern Italian town of Placentia was being held by a small group of young recruits supporting Otho. They were facing off against Vitellius' 30,000-strong Rhine legions. Surely it was a foregone conclusion: a total wipe-out for the Othonians? Actually, no. It is often said that overconfidence breeds arrogance. In this instance the Vitellians were so overconfident that they felt sure they could break down the walls of Placentia despite being roaring drunk and despite having forgotten to bring any siege equipment with them. We can only assume they'd started the victory celebrations before the actual battle. Unsurprisingly, they didn't break in to Placentia.

Punishment

The Roman army is the most disciplined fighting force in the world. This is generally maintained by all that marching, leaving the recruits too knackered for insurrection. However, sometimes harsher methods are called for to maintain unity of spirit.

- For minor offences you might find your pay docked. This veers towards the annoying end of the punishment line. Though it could have major repercussions for you if you cannot pay off accumulated gambling debts or your tab at the local bar.
- A light clubbing. Not to be confused with a heavy clubbing, this is unlikely to lead to your (horrible) death. Every shouty centurion carries a staff in readiness to punish a mild offence with a smack across the shins. If he considers your expression the offence, expect a smack round the head instead. We would recommend a thorough practise of maintaining a neutral face in all circumstances before enlisting in the army.
- Dirty duties. As we've noted every legionary knows his place and role in the legion. Nobody wants that role to be cleaning out the latrines. Particularly the latrines of several thousand Italian lads serving overseas and enthusiastically trying the local cuisine.
- Humiliation. Fail to undertake your duties properly and you might find yourself having to stand all day outside the headquarters holding a ten-foot pole or a pile of mud. And yes,

your comrades-in-arms will be walking past you regularly just to have a good laugh.

- Execution. Dished out for grave derelictions of duty, such as falling asleep on watch duty.
- Decimation. A punishment for the whole community. Soldiers were divided into groups of ten and instructed to pick lots. One legionary in each group of ten would pull out the shortest straw and would be beaten to death with clubs by the other nine. Luckily decimation is very rarely used. The last time was by Emperor Galba in 69 CE.

Chapter 11

Religion and Beliefs

What is the religion of Rome?

Romans worship many gods. The basis of Roman religion is that the gods are ultimately unknowable and must be placated by offerings, sacrifices, prayer and rituals. These are held both publicly, to ensure the survival and fortune of the city itself, and privately by individuals.

What gods are available to worship?

You are in luck. There are hundreds of gods and goddesses to choose from. There are deities available for whatever circumstance you happen find yourself in. For childbirth there is Juno Lucina. On the more fun side there's Edesia, the goddess of food and banquets, or you could pair devotions to Edesia with Bacchus, god of wine, for a truly successful dinner party.

For a trip you might want to think of Abeona, the goddess of outward journeys. En route there is a god for all possible surroundings you might have to travel through: Feronia is the goddess of springs and woods; Neptune is the god of the sea. Oh, and don't forget Adiona, the goddess of safe returns.

Insomniacs are beloved of Somnus, god of sleep. And those who appreciated a good loaf are beloved of Fornax, the goddess of ovens.

Key gods for Rome are Mars, the God of War, and Victoria, goddess of Victory. Jupiter, King of the Gods, has a large temple on the Capitol Hill in Rome, which is certainly worth a visit (before it burns down again).

Ivory statue of Apollo, one of many, many gods available to worship.

That's rather a lot of gods, where shall I start?

Probably a good starting point is with your household gods, the Lares: the Genius and the Penates. Each Roman home has a shrine dedicated to these gods. The Lares care for the homestead: the Genius for the male line of the house and the Penates looked after the food larder. Be sure to take good care of these shrines and their deities lest your roof cave in, your sons prove sterile and there be nothing you fancy to eat for supper.

Aside from ensuring the sanctity of your home and the fertility of your family, we'd recommend timing your god worship by the personal need. Everybody needs the harvest to thrive, so Ceres is a key goddess. With Rome often hit by malaria, Febris goddess of fever is definitely a deity you want on your side. Others you might want to consider honouring are Cupid, god of desire and erotic love, Mercury, god of commerce, and Concordia, goddess of agreement. Absolutely don't forget Cloacina, the goddess of the sewers: it is for the good of all of Rome that we must keep her happy. But really the choice, though baffling, is yours.

The Imperial Cult

I would like to stress that the emperor is not a god. However, his father, brother, sister, niece and son have all been deified,[1] so let us say he is well connected to the gods.

The first man to be made into a god was Julius Caesar, at the behest of his nephew and heir, Augustus. This handily enabled Augustus to call himself the son of a god, which gave him necessary importance points over his arch-rival. Mark Antony. As the son of a god it was inevitable that Augustus would be made a god on his death.

It is important to note that Roman emperors are only declared gods after they are dead. They are not worshipped as gods while living, unlike some dubious parts in the east. Having said that, you can worship the emperor's genius, which is an essence of the emperor, though not actually the emperor.

Being deified is highly dependent on your successor as the job will fall to them. Caligula, not being too fond of his predecessor, Tiberius (because he'd had Caligula's whole family murdered), didn't feel like he could be bothered to make him a god. Similarly, Nero

---

failed to make the divine clouds with his uncle, Claudius, and great-great-grandfather, Augustus, by not having a designated heir and by annoying everyone else who might possibly have made him a god.

With two Flavian emperors deified, it seemed pertinent to build a temple for them. Here you can make offerings to the emperor's deified family members and to the genius of the emperor himself. I'll admit I often take a stroll up to the Quirinal to do exactly that, because when alive Vespasian was very good at keeping his son on the right path. I am convinced he uses that same influence from beyond life.

Rumours that his Imperial Majesty insists on being addressed as our Lord and God are much exaggerated. His Imperial Majesty insists on being addressed by many titles depending on his mood that day. Some days we all feel a bit godlike, don't we?

How do I go about pleasing the gods?

There are two main ways to please your chosen god:

Offerings Everybody likes a present and the gods are no exception. Food is a common offering, including cakes, honey, milk and grains. Wine, known as a libation, can be poured on the floor. Probably best not to offer your best bottle of Falerian, unless you really are in need of the gods' help. It is common for those seeking help from Aesculapius, god of healing, to present a votive model of their ailment. This might be a hand, or an ear, a womb or even hair, for those suffering dreadfully from baldness.

Animal sacrifice Don't worry, you won't be slaughtering sheep in your *insula*. The temples will handle all the necessary arrangements for you: for a fee, naturally. The entrails of the animal are burnt in an altar outside the respective temple. The rest of the meat is then available to buy. On festival days, when mass sacrifices take place, the remaining meat will be available for public banquets. Unless it's a sacrifice to the gods of the underworld,[2] when all the meat is burnt to an inedible, charred lump and nobody gets to eat it. This is known as a holocaust sacrifice.

97

Votive hair!

DID YOU KNOW?

The Emperor Vitellius was so greedy that he couldn't resist stealing meat and cakes from the sacrificial altar and eating them.

How do I know if the Gods are unhappy?

This is a major preoccupation for Romans, to the extent that certain priests are in charge of accessing the gods' level of happiness.

At every animal sacrifice the priest in charge, known as a *haruspex*, will examine the animal's organs. The organs should appear well formed and healthy. If they are deformed in any way, this is an indication that the god is unhappy.

The state also employs augurs who are able to divine the gods' feelings through various signs. These include the flight of birds in the sky, the eating habits of the sacred chickens, weather such as thunder or lightening, and a general pot of 'odd occurrences'.

Augurs are extremely important and powerful. If they declare a bad omen the senate has to disband for the day and cannot sit in assembly. Roman history is awash with instances of bad omens that precipitate grave events. Before Caligula's assassination there were many symbols of impending doom, including several instances of buildings being struck by lightning and a statue of Jupiter that began laughing, to the terror of temple attendants. Julius Caesar's assassination was foreseen by a herd of horses he had once dedicated. They began to cry and refused to eat. The tumbling down of the household gods during a sacrifice by Nero predicted the end of that emperor. When Galba first entered Rome in October 68 CE he was greeted by crowds and a small earthquake that signified that his reign would be short lived.

Not all portents and omens are as extreme as earthquakes and moving statues. Some are a little more mundane, such as the garland that fell off Galba's head and frightened the sacred chickens away. Or when a rooster landed on the shoulder of Vitellius.[2]

Not all omens are a predictor of doom, gloom and beheadings either. There are also good omens. The Emperor Augustus couldn't move for tripping over good omens:

- As an infant he mysteriously vanished and was discovered lying on top of a tower facing the rising sun.
- As a toddler he ordered a noisy frog to stop croaking, and from that day forth no frog ever croaked in that area again.
- As a child he was innocently sitting by the road munching on a crust of bread when an eagle swooped down and nicked it from his hand. Before he could protest, the very same eagle returned the bread to him.
- As a teenager during his coming of age ceremony, his senatorial toga split at the seams and fell to his feet. Bystanders interpreted this as showing that the senatorial order would one day be at his feet.
- As a young man, after Julius Caesar's assassination, Augustus' arrival in Rome brought not only a rainbow above his head but also a spark of lightening that destroyed the tomb of Julius Caesar's daughter. Taking the auspices, twelve vultures appeared to him just as they had to Romulus.
- Before an important battle a fish leaped out of the water and fell to his feet.

All of which, we can agree, must have been quite exhausting for poor Augustus, and anyone within a two-mile radius of him.

The current emperor's father, Vespasian, was similarly plagued by good omens his whole life predicting he would become emperor. While waging war in Judaea he couldn't walk down a street without statues turning around, freak weather conditions and random strangers announcing he would rule the world. In the end he made a bid for emperor just for a bit of peace and quiet.

On a more personal level, if your wife has walked out, your dog is sick, and you've just been fired, that's usually a good indicator that you've annoyed the gods somehow and you need to make amends.

DID YOU KNOW?

Astrology and horoscopes are very popular in Ancient Rome. However, it is considered highly suspect to order a horoscope for somebody else, particularly an emperor.

Are there any specific religious holidays?

No fewer than 135 days in the year are set aside for religious festivals. This is a canny measure for keeping those gods happy, and it's clearly working as Rome remains the dominate force in the known world. To help you navigate the huge number of festivals we've put together a guide.

Festivals to avoid

Though animal sacrifice is normal in ancient Rome, it's a bit icky for the modern visitor. Be warned that all festivals will involve some form of animal death, but you might particularly want to avoid Robigalia, on 25 April, when there is a ritual sacrifice of dogs.

On a similar vein, Fordicidia, on 15 April, involves the sacrifice of pregnant cows to the earth (known as Tellus). And the Ceriala festivities, also in mid-April, include a ritual that consists of foxes with blazing torches tied to them being released into the Circus Maximus.[4]

We recommend that you do not voice your dislike of animal cruelty to any locals, but rather feign an illness to explain your absence from these religious rites.

Festivals worth attending

Megalensia

If you like parades, then the Megalensia is one for you. Beginning on 4 April, it is a six-day extravaganza honouring Cybele. Also known as the 'Great Mother', Cybele was imported from Syria at a time of great strife for the Romans. Accompanying the Great Mother were her priests, the *Galli*. These sprightly little eunuchs are released from their temple on the Palatine Hill once a year to dance down Rome's streets in their colourful saffron gowns, throwing about rose petals and liberally lobbing incense about the place. With their drums and cymbals, they are quite the entourage for the statue of the goddess, who is pulled along in a wooden ship to the Circus Maximus. Once in place, the statue of the goddess will preside over chariot races, plays and other entertainments staged in her honour. For those males of a sensitive nature please also note some of the *Galli* will be flashing knives about as a reminder of their self-castration. You might want to close your eyes and cross your legs until they've danced past.

Parentalia

An unusually private festival, Parentalia is held in February and is dedicated to honouring the dead, most particularly your own relatives. Families take picnics to the tombs of their relatives to share a feast with the deceased. A quiet time that ends with all the family getting together for a slap-up meal together.

DID YOU KNOW?

It is forbidden for any tomb or grave to be within the city walls. The dead have their own city of tombs lining the Appian Road into Rome.

The Festival of Anna Perenna

The festival of Anna Perenna is probably the closest to a modern festival. On the evening of 15 March Romans head to a small patch of green on the Via Flaminia overlooking the river Tiber. Here they pitch their tents close together. They sing songs, make merry and get very drunk. This latter bit is more than just jollity, it is an important religious component. The number of drinks you down foretell the number of years that you have yet to live according to the goddess. Sadly, those most blessed with longevity by the goddess cannot remember it the next morning and are compelled to do the same thing next 15 March. There are no clear instructions on whether a drink counts as a year if you throw it back up again noisily into a bush.

Lupercalia

Should you find yourself surrounded by naked young men fiercely cracking a leather whip in your direction, then we can safely assume one of two things have occurred.

> 1) You've found yourself at one of those 'interesting' parties you heard all about in the Forum this market day.

Or:

> 2) It's Lupercalia.

Lupercalia takes place on 15 February each year. As part of the rites, a dog and some goats are sacrificed on the Palatine Hill on the exact spot where Romulus and Remus were suckled by the she-wolf. The skins of the sacrificed goats are fashioned into leather thongs and attached to handles. These whips are given to a chosen group of young men, whose only qualification for the position is that they be of suitably posh blood. Their sacred duty is to run through the streets naked, whipping young ladies with their goat thongs.

This may sound like an unpleasant assault on young ladies just going about their business, but actually, many of the ladies will purposefully put themselves in the range of a good whipping. This is because to be goat whipped on Lupercalia is said to improve your fertility. It's also an opportunity for a good eyeful of naked young flesh, which is why, come Lupercalia, the streets are swarmed with eager young ladies, their mothers and their grandmothers.

Saturnalia

Taking place from 17–23 December, Saturnalia is a festival of fun, fun, fun. All-out jollity is unleashed in six days of gambling, banqueting, gift giving and role reversals. During Saturnalia the world is turned upside down, with slaves given extra license and freedoms by their masters, including dining with them. It is common for households to elect a King of Saturnalia from their slaves, who will be in a charge for a day and all his commands obeyed.

Though the theme of Saturnalia is one of freedom, it is a brave slave indeed who uses his role as King of the Feast to inflict upon his master the sort of humiliations he himself has dished out to on a daily basis. Let us say the world is turned upside down, but within reason. Still, it is a jolly time for slaves to experience a little bit of what freedom might taste like. There is also the opportunity to try on that Phrygian liberty cap, as it's standard headgear for the festival, whether you be freed, free or enslaved. Colourful tunics are embraced, and the emphasis is on pleasure and fun.

There are no set gifts for handing out at Saturnalia to your nearest and dearest; you can choose whatever you think they might like/deserve. It might be a stylish new writing set, or a broom, or a snow-strainer or even a parrot. You might even think of writing a poem for a gift. Due to everyone being half-cut for most of December, nobody is going to notice how bad your lines are until the New Year at least.[5]

All in all, we recommend throwing yourself wholeheartedly into Saturnalia. Or alternatively take the Seneca route and complain bitterly about how Saturnalia starts earlier and earlier each year. People may curse your lack of spirit but at least you won't be suffering the same killer hangover as the rest of the city.

DID YOU KNOW?

The Delphic Oracle warned Nero to beware of the seventy-third year. Nero assumed this was the age of his death, but actually it was the age of his successor, Galba.

Are there any other religions in Rome?

The number of gods and goddesses available to worship may give the impression that religion is a free for all in Rome, with everyone able to worship whichever deity they like, however they like. This is not the case.

Religion is very much controlled by the state, for it is absolutely crucial to keep the gods placated for the sake of the city and its continuing prosperity.

Therefore, religious activity directed at other, non-Roman gods, is suspect and potentially dangerous, not least because religion generally involves gatherings of people. The state is extremely suspicious of gatherings of people, because gatherings of people can quickly become mobs, and mobs have been known to enthusiastically wreck things. Religious practices are, therefore, tightly controlled by the state.

However, you will find other styles of religion present in Rome. There is a large enough Jewish population to warrant placing a tax on them, as the current emperor has instigated recently. This has led to some unpleasant scenes of elderly men being forcibly undressed to see if they are circumcised and thus taxable.

Toleration for Judaism is variable. Both Tiberius and Claudius expelled the Jewish population from Rome, with Tiberius banning what he saw as 'foreign' religious rites, an edict that also applied to the Egyptian cult of Isis, which had a significant following in Rome.

The current emperor is very particular about maintaining religious rites and we would highly recommend that you do not show any leanings towards foreign beliefs. The emperor has banished his own niece, Domitilla,[6] for converting to that strange Christian cult. He would not hesitate to do the same to you, or worse.

Death of a Vestal

In 90 CE the Emperor Domitian convened the sacred college at his Alban villa. He had a most serious charge to put to them: the Chief Vestal, Cornelia, had broken her vow of chastity. Cornelia was not present to defend herself against the charges and was condemned in her absence. A contemporary of the time, Pliny the Younger, was of the firm view that Domitian undertook this prosecution because he thought such severe adherence to religious practice would add lustre to his reign.

The punishment Cornelia faced was extreme. She was marched through the city to a subterranean vault which she was lowered into. It was then bricked up from the outside, entombing her. She was buried alive.

Morte della Vestale Cornelia

Chief Vestal, Cornelia in her execution cell.

All the way to this horrible death she proclaimed her innocence, entreating Vesta and the other gods to attest that she had done nothing wrong, crying out that she had performed her sacred duties, and that this was proven by Domitian's triumph. This is the reason why the punishment for erring vestals was so severe: breaking their vows was an offence against the gods and the gods might retaliate. The gods, therefore, must be placated. The Romans may claim that they don't practise human sacrifice, but the execution of vestals comes very close to it.

Cornelia's alleged lovers faced the public and painful punishment of being scourged with rods in the Forum, and they too proclaimed their innocence. The scourging was intended to be fatal.

DID YOU KNOW?

Although the Romans believe in ghosts and have festivals such as Parentalia dedicated to the spirits of the departed, they have no set views on an afterlife.

Chapter 12

Law and Order

Rome may have nearly a million inhabitants, but it also has an extremely low recorded crime rate, because there are no mechanisms for recording crime.

How likely am I to be a victim of crime?

With no official statistics available, it's difficult to say, though Juvenal's helpful advice that you make a will before venturing out to dinner after dark, suggests the answer to your question is that it's highly likely. Therefore, you should take proper precautions, such as a decent fleeing speed and the ability to hand over your valuables in an inoffensive manner.

How is Rome policed?

It isn't. There is no official police force in operation. The closest we get to a police force is the *vigiles*, which were formed by Augustus. There are around a thousand *vigiles* spread across the fourteen districts of Rome, but you should be aware that their main function is as firefighters. Fires being an all too common occurrence in Rome, the *vigiles* are charged with spotting and putting out raging infernos before they can spread across the city.

Should the *vigiles* happen to come across you being violently mugged, they may intervene by bashing your attacker on the head with their buckets. However, at the sight of a vague puff of smoke they will happily abandon you to your fate and head towards their main priority.

Elsewhere there are the urban cohorts, who number around 4,000 men. Their main role is in maintaining public order; basically, spotting the exact point at which a crowd becomes a mob, and stepping in to disperse it before it gets too excitable.

The urban cohorts are usually found lurking by the amphitheatres, the theatres and the circus, waiting for an opportunity for mob smashing. They are handy people to have about should your muggers be *en masse*. Elsehow, they might well decide that your brutal fleecing is not disturbing the public order enough for them to intervene.

Alongside the *vigiles* and urban cohorts there is one other armed fighting force, the Praetorian Guard. There are 4,000 of these and they are garrisoned in the Praetorian barracks up on the Viminal Hill. These are the emperor's personal bodyguards, or potential murderers, depending on which mood they've woken up in.[1]

DID YOU KNOW?

The Praetorians have had a hand in many imperial successions. Their Prefect smothered Emperor Tiberius with a pillow to hasten his death and usher in the new emperor, Caligula.

Along with the urban cohorts, the Praetorians form a force to maintain public order, or alternatively disrupt it themselves. We would not recommend asking a Praetorian for assistance. They have far more important things to do than help a citizen.

What should I do if I am the victim of a crime?

Your best bet is to try and sort it out without involving any authorities. Life is much simpler that way. In the case of a theft, you might like to put a notice up offering a reward for your lost item, such as this one from Pompeii: 'A copper pot went missing from my shop. Anyone who returns it to me will be given 65 bronze coins (sestertii). 20 more will be given for information leading to the capture of the thief.'[2]

If this elicits no responses, you might make casual enquiries in the neighbourhood as to whether anyone knows who the culprit is. This being Rome, and gossip being one of the main pastimes, it is likely that someone knows the villain. Once identified, you can now go and recover your property. We would recommend taking some tough mates with you. Alternatively, if violence upsets you (in which case why are you in Rome?) you might want to use the patron system. Your patron has more clout than you, and possibly even tougher mates. He can make suitable enquiries, lean on the right people and hopefully get your property back to you. If human intervention cannot return your property, it may well be time to get the gods involved via a stonking good curse: 'Not let him sleep or have children now or in the future until he brings my cloak to the temple of her divinity.'[3]

Upsetting the Emperor

The emperor is the most powerful man in all the empire. On his word continents are invaded, populations are expelled, and men are killed. It is, therefore, quite important to not get on his bad side. However, even for a seasoned palace insider like myself, it is easy to stumble into offending his Imperial Majesty. Here are just some of the ways people have managed to upset an emperor:

- Plotting to replace him as emperor.
- Being a member of his family who might make a better emperor than him.
- Being related to someone who was emperor twelve years before the current emperor was emperor.[4]
- Being with an emperor who was emperor thirteen years before the current emperor was emperor and helping him to commit suicide.[5]
- Sexual shenanigans with one of his relatives. Most particularly upsetting, and lethal for you, if it turns out to be his wife.[6]
- Marrying his ex-wife or having previously been married to his current wife. With added upset factor for making a joke about it.[7]
- Writing a play about Caesar's killers, Brutus and Cassius.
- Being descended from Brutus and Cassius.
- Accusing the emperor of fixing the result of a gladiator match.
- Booing the Blues chariot team.

- Being tall and handsome.
- Being arrogant.
- Possessing a purple cloak that was once admired by some people.
- Stealing a peacock from the imperial aviary.
- Writing a play whose plotline is a bit similar to the emperor's recent divorce.
- Writing a play in which the Greek mythical king, Agamemnon, doesn't come out well.
- Winning an election and the announcer having a slip of the tongue and declaring you emperor rather than consul.
- Being born during some unusual weather activity that some might say was a portent.
- Naming your slave Hannibal.
- Carrying a coin with the image of a deified emperor into the toilet with you.[8]
- Changing outfits near to a statue of a deified emperor.

The Emperor Domitian, a man not to upset.

How do I make sure the guilty is suitably punished?

As Rome lacks any kind of public prosecutor or investigatory force, a crime is not a crime unless someone makes a public accusation of one. You can do this by making your accusation to the local magistrate, generally a Praetor. Obviously, you will need a person to accuse. Both you and the defendant will be summoned to appear before the official. He will decide if there is a case to answer. If so, a judge will be appointed, and a trial will be arranged for a few days' time.

This is where the fun begins. Roman trials are held in the open air with a healthy number of eager spectators. As there is no police force in Rome, justice and punishment need to be shown publicly as a deterrent. It also passes as entertainment, so the more novel/grievous the offence the bigger the crowd you can expect.

Don't worry if your case is on the more mundane side, because spectators are available to hire. Given the right financial incentive they will gasp, cheer and applaud at the right moments to aid your case most.[9] This can be handy as trials can be very, very long. The prosecution is allotted six hours to speak and the defence nine hours. Do not be fooled into thinking this is just a maximum: lawyers will, and do, speak for the whole time.[10] A financial incentive to stay the full day is imperative to maintain a good healthy level of applause.

What kinds of punishments are available for those found guilty of a crime?

Without an organised police force rooting out crime, the emphasis is on deterrence, which is why some Roman punishments may seem a little on the extreme side. The earliest set of laws in Rome date back to the beginnings of the Republic. Known as the Twelve Tables, they list some of the punishments meted out for crimes. For instance, if found guilty of burning down a barn or destroying a grain supply you faced being burnt alive. Anyone daring to let their livestock pasture on a neighbour's crops faced hanging; from which we might deduce that early Roman society was a seething mass of feuding farmers who had to be kept in line by the threat of grievous punishments.

There are prisons, but these are only to hold the guilty prior to punishment. What your punishment is depends on both your crime and your social class. Slaves and persons of free status face different punishments for the exact same crime.

DID YOU KNOW?

If a slave murders his master all the slaves in the household face execution; even if they have no part in the murder.

As a Roman citizen you can't be tortured or flogged or crucified, which is a relief. You can also appeal to the emperor. He doesn't have to listen or see you, but should you succeed, emperors do love to show off their clemency, which could work in your favour.

You'll be pleased to know that most crimes are resolved by the handing over of money. You might be fined for theft or damaging another's property, and this includes his slaves. We'd advise a strong line on not touching other people's slaves, no matter how insolent they are to you.

Other punishments of the non-lethal kind include flogging. A free person gets a slightly better deal by facing only an excruciating beating with rods, whereas a slave can expect the more painful lash.

More serious offences might see you consigned to hard labour, or worse, sent to the mines. This is a truly awful fate that will undoubtedly result in your death.

DID YOU KNOW?

The Roman punishment for patricide is quite bizarre. The culprit was sewn up in a leather sack with a dog, a monkey, a snake and a cockerel, then rolled into the river.

Execution wise, though the free citizen escapes crucifixion and torture, he doesn't escape being beaten to death, burnt alive, decapitation or death by an arena full of wild beasts. The slave can console himself with the knowledge that, since Tiberius' time, his master is obliged to try him officially before he can be consigned to death by leopard.

Punishments for the Elite

Brace yourselves because this is going to upset you. One of the punishments the elite face is the renunciation of the emperor's friendship. This is stinging, though obviously not as stinging as a leopard eating your face. As a punishment it taps into the elite's pride and sense of civic duty and acts as a public shaming. Roman life being lived out in the open and very publicly, being denied access to the emperor or excluded from certain events is pretty damning. It announces to all the city your lack of honourable qualities. Whether your friends or clients will want to be associated with such an undesirable remains to be seen. It may well be in their best interest to avoid you. Your career is certainly going nowhere without the emperor's support, and that of the rest of the elite.

The other punishment we hear a lot about in relation to the upper classes is exile from Rome. This could be temporary or permanent. It might be a comfy exile or a very uncomfortable exile, but you at least get advance notice and a chance to gather your things together before leaving the city.

DID YOU KNOW?

Famous names who were exiled from Rome include orator Cicero, poets Ovid and Juvenal and numerous members of the imperial family, including the current empress.[11]

Romans are pretty much uniformly in agreement that Rome is the centre of the world and the only place to be, so being made to leave your beloved city is quite heart-wrenching. It also entirely excludes you from the political system, as well as society. Maybe you'll be able to pick up your life on your return, presuming yours is a temporary exile, or maybe your name will be forever tainted. And for those languishing outside the city gates still, will anyone remember who you are?

If you're thinking how jolly unfair it is that the wealthy of Rome can go about committing crimes and if they get caught go and relax in their seaside villa for a bit, you are probably right. However, the elite did face another type of punishment that was more exacting than exile: suicide by imperial decree (sometimes referred to as a free choice of death). Of course, it's not really a free choice of death, it's more a case of 'go execute yourself, so we don't have to worry about the mess'. It's also a good way of avoiding one of those seven-hour speech trials. But it's really bloody annoying to receive such a missive from the emperor, especially when you were actually expecting an imperial dinner invitation.

You might choose to emulate Nero's top party organiser and arbiter of taste, Petronius, in your death. He slit his wrists, but then repeatedly bound up his veins to further converse with his friends at a special farewell party. Over a period of several hours he also noted down every one of Nero's debaucheries to be delivered to the emperor personally after his death.

Chapter 13

Politics

How can I be involved in politics?

Given that Rome is effectively a monarchy,[1] you may wonder how much you, as an ordinary Roman, can be involved in politics. The answer is, a surprising amount.

If you are a male citizen, you have a vote. Roman citizens are divided into tribes, and then centuries within tribes, and then into property classes within the centuries. These divisions are given a certain number of votes to cast in the election of public officials.

Don't underestimate the power this vote gives you. There is tremendous pressure placed on the sons of the elite to climb the pole of power by securing key electable positions, such as aedile and quaestor. The competition is fierce, which is great news for the ordinary Roman citizen, since come election time the posh boys are desperate for your vote.

Elections are, therefore, a unique time when the elite are suddenly struck with a desire to get on with the common plebs. They are likely to be in the Forum most days in the run-up to the vote, making nice speeches and radiating appeal. They will even have hired a nomenclator[2] to whisper your name to them, so they can greet you as if they know you personally. The aim is to convince you into believing this would-be official is your best bud in the city and the only man standing who has your best interests at heart.

This is your opportunity. Obviously, blatant bribery in elections is against the law, but not blatant granting of favours. This falls under the patron/client code of conduct, whereby a group of men, who are coincidentally all standing for election in the near future, suddenly decide they all need many more clients, perhaps hundreds more.

The rich man cares little for the poor man the rest of the year, so do not miss this great opportunity to make use of his influence. The good news is that he is sure to help. Candidates are often keen to prove that they hold a full house of noble Roman attributes, one of which is generosity. Get in there and enjoy public banquets aplenty, free distributions of grain and actual coinage pressed in your hand.

DID YOU KNOW?

In the consular elections of 53 BCE two candidates were prepared to fork out 10 million sesterces to win the support of the people.

How do I vote?

Voting is done outdoors, which might be nice on a sunny day but less so on more inclement days. You will need to get yourself over to either the Forum or the Campus Martius, and quickly, for there is not nearly enough room to accommodate all of Rome's eligible voters. Voting is done within your tribe, with the majority votes in that tribe being put forward as the group's decision. Voting takes place *en masse* and in order of property class, so the richest vote first and the poorest last.

Cicero, in proper pontification pose.

115

Back in the Republic votes were delivered verbally, but that was deemed too open to public intimidation and so now everyone votes in secret by writing their preferred candidate's name on a wax tablet.

> **DID YOU KNOW?**
>
> In an attempt to stop election bribery, Augustus personally forked out 1,000 sesterces for each member of a particular voting tribe to stop them seeking payment from the candidates.

If I don't have a vote can I still be involved in politics?

Absolutely. Remember the electoral candidates will be presenting themselves in the Forum each day to explain why they should be voted into office. This is your perfect opportunity for a good heckle. Heckle well and you diminish them in the public eye and thwart their election chances. Or shout the loudest over the hecklers and you might well win the election for them.

Another way to get involved and sway the election result is persuasion via graffiti. A common sight in Rome around election time is the multitude of adverts scrawled on walls promoting the various candidates. Sometimes people will put names to their ads so you can see what notable citizen supports which candidate. Get involved by scrawling your own endorsement (ideally use your own wall or else get the homeowner's permission first. Or just run really, really quickly). This kind of endorsement is not limited to the eligible voting population of Rome: women often put their names to preferred candidates, as do groups of people. Election posters in Pompeii name groups based on professions, such as fishermen, onion sellers, barbers and even prostitutes. There are also inscriptions claiming that the poor and the destitute prefer a certain candidate.

> **DID YOU KNOW?**
>
> Of the 25,000 inscriptions and graffiti found in Pompeii, 2,500 relate to elections.

If I'm unhappy with an official what can I do about it?

Don't vote for him next time he stands for election. Or alternatively, you might want to take more direct action. Future emperor, Vespasian, when serving as governor of Africa, was pelted with turnips by the locals. Emperor Claudius had stale bits of bread lobbed at him from citizens annoyed by a grain shortage. Even Augustus, as a young man, found himself under attack from civilians armed with stones who were displeased at his war against the renegade pirate, Sextus Pompey.

If that seems a little too violent a way to air a grievance[3] there are more peaceful methods. Why not attend the Games or the circus and yell your complaint to the emperor himself? Or make up an offensive ditty to sing at him as a way of showing how annoyed you are at him.

DID YOU KNOW?

When Nero divorced his wife, Octavia, the public vocalised their disgust every time the emperor went out. Similar public pressure made Domitian recall Domitia from exile.

Political violence

In the late Republican period using violence became the norm in politics. By the 50s BCE it had become a standard tactic by politicians to employ their own mobs. Not only was this a great way to increase employment for the local population (in particular out-of-work gladiators), it also allowed you to prevent people voting against the law you want to pass.

Pompey the Great used his mob to pour a basket of manure over the head of the consul, Bibulus, and clear the Forum of his opponents. This was how his land law was passed. However, Pompey soon became the target of Clodius' mob. They followed Pompey about the city and heckled all of his speeches with such gems as: 'What do you call a man in search of another man? Pompey!' and 'What do you call a man who scratches his head with one finger? Pompey!'[4] Clearly

---

there was a hurtful element of truth in these heckles, since Pompey got super touchy about it and decided he would stay home rather than ever go to the Forum again. Though he might also have been influenced by that time Clodius sent someone to assassinate him.

Such was the level of violence that a simple thing like electing the *aediles* for the year set off a battle in the Forum of the various mobs, with several people losing their lives in the bloody fighting. The elections of 53 BCE, when Clodius was standing for praetor and his arch mob rival, Milo, for consul, had to be abandoned due to full-scale warfare on the streets.

One day in 52 BCE Clodius and Milo (and their armed mobs) happened to meet on the Appian way. It all kicked off big time and Clodius was killed. His supporters in their rage burnt down the senate house and intimidated poor Cicero so much he was unable to deliver his closing speech at Milo's murder trial. Without Cicero's silver tongue Milo was found guilty and exiled.

Acknowledgments

Special thanks to Simon Walpole who designed the brilliant timelines and map, and who so fabulously made sense of my extremely vague and badly worded ideas. To Carol Klio Burrell who did such a wonderful job envisaging Hortensia and Ajax. I fell instantly in love with every sketch she sent to me and I am in awe of her talent. To Scott Rowland for the kind use of his holiday snaps. To Phoebe Harkins and her magical librarian powers of selecting the exact book I required at every odd moment.

Classics Twitter is a treasure trove of experts and I received some key help while writing this book. A special mention goes to Dr Sophie Hay, Dr Virginia Campbell and Dr Jane Draycott for their assistance in answering my, sometimes stupid, questions. Also to Dr Rob Cromaty for endeavouring to find an interesting story about mosaics.

Special mention also to the Roman and Byzantine History Facebook group members who answered so many of my quick queries with helpful/ thoughtful suggestions.

Notes

Welcome to Ancient Rome

1 Genuine Roman punishment. See the chapter on Law and Order for further (horrible) details.
2 Pliny, *Natural History* VII.130
3 Falerian is considered the best of Roman wine. It's also the priciest.
4 The poet Virgil, in his work *The Aeneid*, has a chapter where Aeneas is shown a vision of the future glory and majesty of Rome. Amazingly, this doesn't encourage him to sneakily found Rome himself and get all that glory for himself.
5 Vesta was the goddess of the home and hearth. The Vestal Virgins were her priestesses. Their key duty was to keep the eternal flame of Vesta burning and guard it at all times.
6 Roman gods are always taking sides in wars, getting mortal women up the duff and generally ruining people's lives. They are not a bit sorry for it.
7 Roman myths are awash with shepherds stumbling over abandoned babies to the extent that it must have seriously impeded their sheep work, though it was an easy and cheap source of labour.
8 Though claims that it is the original are somewhat undermined by casual references to replacement walls, floors and ceilings being fitted. Perhaps the door is original. Or maybe the door knocker.
9 Livy, *The History of Rome* I.5
10 This is not normal in the world of city founding. Rome is unique in filling its walls with outsiders from its very beginnings. Those outsiders being very male led to an incident referred to, unpleasantly, as 'The Rape of the Sabine Women'. There are no words that can make this incident less repulsive.

11 Livy records in his *History of Rome* that Romulus fought against the Sabines, the Crustumiums, the Laviniums, the Fidenates and the Veintes. Busy chap.

12 Livy, *History of Rome* 1.59

13 The Carthaginian general, Hannibal, famously crossed the Alps into Italy with his elephants and created general mayhem. The Roman strategy, led by Fabius Maximus, was to ignore them and hope they went away. Which they did, amazingly, and it was Round 2 to the Romans.

14 Mary Beard, in her book *SPQR*, estimates that by the end of the fourth century BCE Rome likely had half a million soldiers it could call up. Which is quite a fighting force.

15 Equestrians are the second rank down from Senators and, apparently, can form a mob at least as good as the plebeian equivalent.

16 They also won support because they could shower their soldiers with booty from Rome's continuing expansion and were pretty good at making inspiring speeches.

17 The most lasting of Caesar's reforms was that of the calendar, which had fallen hopelessly out of sync with the seasons. He standardised the length of the twelve months.

18 Caesar being the ultimate populares, had left the people 75 drachma each in his will and his garden for everyone to enjoy. Which was nice. Unsurprisingly, the people were somewhat annoyed at Caesar's murderers, perhaps anticipating further bribery from the Dictator.

19 Which is inspirational if you're under thirty and downright depressing if you're not.

20 The Praetorian Prefect was head of the emperor's own bodyguard, the Praetorian Guard. Sejanus was far from the last Prefect to get above himself; they were to cause trouble and chaos in Rome down the centuries. Sejanus himself suffered a bloody end when Tiberius finally got wind of his dastardliness. He was executed and every single one of his statues destroyed.

21 Though a large number of people were involved in the plot to kill Caligula, and all for very sound reasons (i.e. we don't want a mad emperor), it was actually all kicked off by a certain Cassius Chaerea. Chaerea's motivation was that he had a rather high-pitched voice and Caligula kept making bad jokes about it. Compared to Brutus the Liberator and Brutus the Caesar killer, Caligula's assassination is distinctly lacking in a nobility of spirit.

22 The Julio Claudian dynasty is one big poison fest. Claudius' hapless son, Britannicus, was spectacularly poisoned at an imperial banquet in front of everyone. Tiberius' son, Drusus, was poisoned by dastardly Sejanus. Caligula tried to nobble the chariot races by poisoning both the horses and the charioteers of rival teams. Nero poisoned his aunt with an extra strong laxative.

23 Women allegedly gave birth during Nero's poetry recitals. It's not entirely unfeasible that the baby was conceived during the same recital; they were very long.

24 Explosive diarrhoea. Messy.

25 The Jewish Wars, which both Vespasian and Titus took part in, were a messy cleaning up of a Judaean uprising. Hundreds of thousands of Jews were killed and the temple of Jerusalem was destroyed. Those rebels who survived found themselves enslaved, and many were transported to Rome to labour. Titus, therefore, is for many, less of a war hero and more of a war criminal.

26 Mount Vesuvius, previously thought to be a mountain, spectacularly revealed herself to be a volcano in 79 CE, destroying Pompeii, Herculaneum and several other settlements. Titus was considerably upset by this disaster and personally arranged disaster relief to the survivors of the eruption.

27 It is always politic to be polite about the current emperor. Once he's dead feel free to spit at his busts, wee on his statues and write appalling poetry about his supposed kinks. Though it's best to wait for the official verdict before undertaking any such protests. It may be the emperor is unexpectedly made into a god, which means you have just broken religious protocol in drastic fashion. Men have faced treason trials for much, much less (such as having a wee with a coin baring the portrait of the emperor in your pocket).

28 Juvenal, *Satire* III.232

29 Most recently in 80 CE, but also, in 83 BCE and in 69 CE. These two were the result of civil unrest, as opposed to a rogue thunderbolt from resident god, Jupiter.

30 As a dating system this is complicated by the fact that not all consuls serve the whole year. Titus Flavius Clemens won't serve the whole of his term as he's executed for atheism before the end of the year.

31 Domitian is far from the first emperor to have months named after him. August is named after Augustus and July after Julius Caesar.

Both Caligula and Nero changed the names of months, though these, like Domitian's, ultimately, did not stick.

32 As Praetorian Prefect, Sejanus did. He named the boy Paezon, which translates as 'Boy Toy'.

33 The name Octavian took after finding out Julius Caesar had adopted him as his son in his will. To show his gratitude, Octavian made Julius Caesar into a god: Divi Filius means 'son of a god'. This was a handy tool in his decade-long war of one-upmanship with Mark Antony.

34 The unfortunate cognomen given to Fabius Maximus by his (loving?) parents, as he had a wart on his upper lip. Fabius Maximus was a bit of a cognomen attracter as his parents also named him Ovicula, meaning 'Lambkin', because of his calm nature. For hapless Warty Lambkin there really was no choice but to become a successful general, which he did in the Second Punic War.

35 Marcus Tullius Cicero was an orator and lawyer in the first century BCE. He's very quotable, 'If you have a garden and a library, you have everything you need' being a good one.

36 Both characters from Greek myth. Narcissus famously fell in love with his own reflection. Pallas was the Titan god of warfare.

Chapter 1: Social Structure

1 Though, interestingly, the chariot races have no such restrictions re gender segregation.

2 The *cursus honorum* positions start with the post of *quaestor*, followed by *aedile*, *praetor* and consul. A son from a good family would be expected to work their way through each of these positions, but it is not a given that they will. All posts are elected, and the voting public can be notoriously fickle. They will also be against some strong competition from other sons of good families. There is much honour attached to following the *cursus honorum* and much dishonour for anyone who does not.

3 A prejudice that seemed firmly rooted in the fact that Gauls wear trousers. This more than anything else is seen as the mark of a barbarian. We firmly advise you leave your trouser wear at home.

4 The Emperor Domitian has – perhaps unfairly – a legacy of persecuting senators. He didn't execute nearly as many as other

emperors, which is admittedly not very comforting for today's senators, who would obviously prefer not to be executed at all.

5 Book six in Pliny the Elder's *Natural History* includes a chapter entitled: 'The decay of morality is caused by the produce of the sea', which seems a little unfair on the mullet.

6 The exception is the philosopher, Epictetus whose master was himself a former slave of Emperor Nero. Epictetus wrote on philosophy and makes scant mention of his former slave status. It should be noted that, as well as freedmen owning slaves, slaves often owned slaves.

7 Nero's mum, Agrippina, did not approve of her son's infatuation with the freedwoman and worked hard to end the liaison. It didn't entirely work because, though Nero dutifully married a more suitable wife, Acte continued to act as his mistress, and was present at his funeral.

8 Callistus, Caligula's private secretary, was instrumental in helping smooth the path of his hideously bloody murder. Similarly, without the help of Claudius' food taster, Halotus, it is unlikely those poisoned mushrooms would ever have made it into the imperial tummy. The imperial staff's easy access to the emperor will have big consequences in a year's time for Emperor Domitian. But for now, he is blissfully ignorant of his freedmen's intentions.

9 *Natural History*, vii.36.

10 Ridiculously, Clodius' new adopted father was many years younger than him. As with many of the Tribune of the Plebs in the Republican era, Clodius was horribly murdered.

11 Spartacus, a Thracian gladiator, led one of the only slave revolts in Roman history. He put together an army of 70,000 slaves. The fear of a repeat of Spartacus is what lies behind many of the draconian rules and punishments aimed at slaves.

12 A case makes it into the law books regarding a freedman whose slave job was as a dancer. It is ruled that should his master want a bit of a dance to watch, the freedman is obligated to perform free of charge for him, and also at any of his former master's friends' dance parties. Obligations do extend to, though not necessarily, sexual favours.

13 Ajax is not boasting here. He genuinely is very important, which any would-be client needs to know. Rome is not for the humble. To get along, expect much discourse along the lines, 'Don't you know who I am?', and then their full CV, which will aid you in weighing up whether they are worth being friends with.

14 For a very good account of how Roman *amicus* work dip into Pliny the Younger's letters. To the modern readers it seems that Pliny is constantly boasting to friends about how much he has done for them over the years and soliciting a 'well done, Pliny, aren't you a marvel' style love-in. But this is *amicitia* at work: list the favours you have bestowed before launching into the favour you require (and Pliny is generally asking for a favour on behalf of someone else). See also Martial, who writes a series of poems to Domitian's freedman chamberlain, Parthenius, hoping he'll put his poetry in front of the emperor.

Chapter 2: Family

1 There are very few examples of this happening. What examples we do have date way back to the age of the kings, so there is some doubt as to their authenticity. Murdering your relatives was, technically, legally possible but it seems unlikely that it did happen.

2 In a neat use of *amicitia*, Otho inserts himself into the imperial court by pretending to fall in love with an imperial freedwoman many, many years his senior. Otho benefits from this liaison by an introduction to the court, while the nameless imperial freedwoman presumably benefits in other ways.

3 Julia's education included learning how to spin and weave, never saying anything undignified (for it would be recorded in the household diary) and never to fraternise with strangers, particularly of the male variety.

4 Women are not the only victims of Juvenal's criticism. He hates everybody. Unreservedly.

5 Such as Cato the Elder, who lived in the second century BCE. Cato believed sex was a good cure for lazy slaves and permitted them to sleep with his female slaves, for a price. Obviously, the female slaves had no say in this enterprise. Fearful that his slaves might conspire against him, he worked hard on fomenting distrust amongst them. They were whipped with leather straps for the smallest mistake. For more serious offences he had his slave tried in front of their fellow slaves and then put them to death. Those elderly slaves for which he had no more use he would get rid of, selling them for a few

coins. Even Cato's biographer, Plutarch (writing 300 years later) is aghast at his attitude towards his slaves and makes it clear just how loathsome he finds it.

6 Martial is absolutely horrified by one Ponticus cutting out his slave's tongue and crucifying him: 'Don't you realize, man. Though he can't speak, the rest of us can?' Epigrams: 2.67.

7 The Romans link many factors to climate, including health and personality. See the chapter on health on medicine for further details on what it means for your wellness. Essentially, those from the chilly northern bit of Europe are thought to be extremely brave fighters, but wild, which is why they don't have what the Romans consider proper governments. People from the warmer east and southern countries are thought to be clever, docile (and thus easy to rule) and a bit lazy. Rome, naturally, with a climate in between these extremes, produces the best of all people for personality and abilities.

8 Roman doctor, Soranus, in his book on gynaecology, has a helpful checklist of what to look out for in a baby to ensure that it is worth spending time raising it.

9 Girls can be an expensive luxury. You can't send them out to work in as many professions and you have to fork out on a dowry when they marry. For this reason, families who already have a girl, or are in dire need of an additional income, may decide to expose a baby girl.

10 As current emperor, Domitian, has recently done.

11 Another extremely unpleasant aspect of Roman slavery. The free, easy, availability of sex within the household meant that Roman males could pursue their desires elsewhere, which in turn helped limit a wife's pregnancies.

Chapter 3: Clothing

1 According to top Roman gossip, Suetonius, Caligula was fond of wearing both women's robes and women's shoes. He also liked to dress up as the goddess Venus. Suetonius tells us, somewhat disapprovingly, that Caligula, 'Paid no attention to traditional or current fashions in his dress; ignoring male conventions, and even human decencies.' We assume the latter is referring to the Venus outfit.

2 Cloaks can be very fancy. A friend of the poet Martial somehow managed to spend 10,000 sesterces on his cloak. One can only imagine it was made from gold thread and studded with jewels for that price.

3 Naturally they were home-woven by his long-suffering female relatives.

4 Recent research has suggested that the Flavian lady hairdo might well have been sewn into place and that the towering front curls might, in reality, be a fierce bit of back combing. For further information, I'd recommend checking out historical hairdresser, Janet Stephens, on YouTube.

5 Hortensia is wise not to use white-lead face powder. The effects of lead on the skin are well known: it causes the very blemishes it seeks to cover, also hair loss and, in extreme cases, death.

6 Ochre is a type of clay. With the red variety being popular with Roman ladies for lipstick and rouge.

7 Malachite is a mineral. For blue eyeshadow the Romans used Azurite, another mineral.

8 The *toga virilis* is the standard toga type. It is plain white and donned by boys entering adulthood, around the age of seventeen, in a ceremony at the Temple of Mars Ultor.

Chapter 4: Accommodation

1 Though probably best not to assume living in such a crowded city will necessarily result in a busy social life. The poet Martial is most annoyed that his neighbour, Novius, pays him no attention. As he says: 'If you don't want to see Novius, you should live next door. Or better still, in the same house on the same floor.' Epigrams 1.86.

2 Don't feel too sorry for Seneca. He has another house outside of Rome, and lots of friends with big houses, and enough money to buy effective ear plugs.

3 Romans have a heavy suspicion of gatherings of groups of people. This is not surprising given Rome's history and the propensity of the locals to form mobs when they get ticked off about things. Cookshops hold a suspicious number of people in a single place and have found themselves closed down entirely in order to keep the peace, as the Emperor Claudius once ordered.

4 The *Amores* is Ovid's take on the art of love. It may have led to the poet's exile under the Emperor Augustus. It is certainly not the

sort of book you should wish to associate with given the current emperor's stance on morality.

5   If you cannot afford a rotating ceiling, why not tell your guests you have one anyway. If you supply them with enough wine, they are likely to see your whole dining room rotate.

6   Be sure to stress to your guests that this is a warning against vanity, as opposed to a comment on any particular member of your household.

7   Domitian's love of solitude was considered greatly suspicious by the Romans. So much so that somebody invented a story that he was spending his time alone stabbing flies with the sharp end of his pen, which, even if true, is scarcely indicative of a dubious personality.

Chapter 5: Shopping

1   From Shakespeare's *Julius Caesar*.

2   See the Politics chapter for more info on Publius Clodius.

3   According to Cicero in his Philippic speeches. In the same speech he accuses Mark Antony of having prostituted himself in his youth and being a dreadful lush of a drunk.

4   Including Cicero, whose head and hands Mark Antony displayed on the rostra, as a lesson for anyone else who might care to remind him of that night he got hideously drunk.

5   It won't be good for either the Vestals or Rome if it has been extinguished.

6   Though this is still under construction and will end up being named the Forum of Nerva after Domitian's successor. Pah.

7   *Silvae*, 1.1.

8   Hortensia is quite correct in this. With no refrigeration available, perishable goods are pretty much going to perish en route.

9   The grain ships from Egypt are considered so crucial that that blockading them is considered a good tactic in pressurising Rome, as African governor, Clodius Macer, attempted during the year 69 CE. It was also going to be the tactic of Emperor Vespasian to defeat Vitellius. However, his general 'Beaky' Antonius Primus got overexcited and invaded Italy before the plan could be enacted.

10   According to Pliny the Elder, who also makes mention of the griffins in Scythia who apparently also collect gold.

11 See the chapter on Health and Medicine for a further explanation behind this.

12 Dark-skinned Africans are referred to as Ethiopians in our sources.

13 Pliny the Elder seems very surprised by Ethiopians, disclaiming that nobody would have believed in them if they had not witnessed them with their own eyes. Which seems slightly odd given that Rome had a blooming trade with Africa. Maybe Pliny didn't get out much.

Chapter 6: Food and Drink

1 Pliny, *Natural History* ix.76.

2 *Geoponica* 20.46.1-5.

3 Should you want further things to do with a dormouse, and who wouldn't, you might consider dipping them in honey and poppy seeds. Petronius, *Satyricon* 6.31.

4 Suetonius, *Life of Claudius* 40.

5 Herculaneum (bar/inn joined to the maritime baths); 10675.

6 Pliny, *Natural History* xiii.25. Frankly, Pliny is equally as dumbfounded by this latest innovation, and perfume in general, which he describes as 'the most pointless of all luxuries'.

7 Pliny, *Natural History* ix.19. Though don't try this at home. Scholars have and it doesn't work.

8 Martial, *Epigrams* 2.18, who happily admits to being both a spaniel and a toad in his pursuit of an invitation.

9 Suetonius, *Life of Claudius* 32.

10 Suetonius, *Life of Vitellius* 13.

11 Pliny the Younger, *Letters* 1.15, who suggests his friend, Clarus, has blown off his dinner invitation to instead attend a party with 'Spanish dancing-girls', which admittedly does sound a lot more fun than spending an evening with Pliny.

Chapter 7: Entertainment

1 The Gaetulians were from North Africa.

2 Pre emperors, the Games were organised by individuals, generally the *aediles* for that year. Put on a good show and the people might well

remember it when you are next up for election. Equally, putting on a terrible show might well scupper your career. This is evident by Pliny the Elder listing the names of the officials who were the first to display elephants or lions or hippos in their games hundreds of years later.

3 A *lanista* is the owner of a gladiator training school.

4 Examining the results of gladiator fights in Pompeii, Mary Beard and Keith Hopkins, in their book on the Colosseum, estimate a gladiator had a one in five chance of being killed in any one match.

5 New animals to Rome are a particular favourite with Augustus proudly showing a rhino. Galba was the first to introduce Romans to the spectacle of tightrope-walking elephants. Whereas Sulla first introduced mass lion fights, with 100 beasts facing off against each other in the arena.

6 Emperors have repeatedly tried to introduce extra teams to spread the love a bit more. Most recently, Domitian has added the gold and purple teams. Like renaming the months, these changes rarely stick, and the Blues, Greens, Whites and Reds continue to be the standard chariot teams.

7 These included acting, lyre playing and singing, as well as chariot racing. Nero was a man with a lot of hobbies.

8 Martial, *Epigrams* 7.xxxiv.

Chapter 8: Health and Medicine

1 Some historians think this may be asthma.

2 There are various competing theories about Claudius' illness, from Tourette's to cerebral palsy.

3 Vestal Virgins would therefore make excellent bounty hunters of runaway slaves. There is no evidence, sadly, that any ever took up this profession.

4 See also statues of the god Priapus with his grossly oversized erect member.

5 As Pliny the Elder puts it: 'Only a doctor can kill a man with impunity'. *Natural History* xxxix.18.

6 Because they are considered clever people. See also secretaries and teachers. This cleverness is both admired by the Romans and considered very suspicious.

7 Some doctors, in an attempt to drum up business, would give public demonstrations of their craft.

8 To dream of a flowing river indicates good health. To dream of an abnormally fast and full-flowing river denotes you have too much blood. To dream of a rough sea indicates bowel troubles. To have one of those dreams where you are running away from something terrifying suggests dehydration.

9 For that all-important wind direction.

10 The Hippocratic writings from Greece record these detailed observations as the patients' condition changed from each day to the next. A disturbing number conclude with, 'on the 4th day, died'.

11 Though Pliny crucially omits whether the onion should be chopped up or whole before being shoved up your rear end.

12 Pliny the Elder also notes it has been used in suicides by those suffering unbearable agonies of the body.

Chapter 9: Work

1 See Suetonius, *Life of Nero* 47. He quotes Nero's words in detail and helpfully records all those times on his final journey that the soon-to-be-dead emperor was really, really annoying. This is proof, if proof be needed, that someone who was there at the time has had a good vent about it.

2 Whether the Parthians really thought they had Nero, or whether they saw it as an opportunity to needle Rome, is open to interpretation. The Parthians and Romans periodically would have a bit of a scrap over who owned Armenia, including a war under Nero's reign. This was settled by a big old party in Rome where the new agreed king of Armenia was crowned. For the scale of this celebration it's worth noting Nero spent 800,000 sesterces per day on it.

3 As the poet, Martial, repeatedly begs Domitian's chamberlain, Parthenius, to do.

4 Statius, *Silvae* VI.3.

5 Martial, *Epigrams* 8.XI.

6 See the chapter 'Welcome to Ancient Rome' for an account of Warty Lambkin, aka Quintus Fabius Maximus Verrucosus.

7 The man in question is the arch-enemy of Pliny the Younger, Regulus. Pliny is regularly critical of Regulus, rightfully in this case. Although his jibes that Regulus is overdoing the mourning of his son veer towards the spiteful side.

Chapter 10: Warfare

1 All the figures quoted should be considered rough. Roman historians are notorious for quoting improbable numbers of soldiers in battle. However, a lot of Romans must have been killed, given how tetchy and sensitive they still are to mentions of Cannae.
2 Victor Davis Hanson in *The Reader's Companion to Military History*.
3 Modern-day Turkey, which in the first century comprised many different provinces.
4 Modern-day Iran/Iraq. The Parthians had their own empire that backed onto Rome's and included Mesopotamia and Babylon as part of its territory.
5 Special mention to the Parthian's most impressive fighting tactic: the infamous Parthian Shot. The trick was to appear as if retreating. The enemy forces would then pursue the Parthian horsemen and quickly discover their secret talent: firing arrows backwards over their shoulders. It is where we get the English phrase 'a parting shot'.
6 Yes, that Cassius. The one who, along with Brutus and many others, would assassinate Julius Caesar.
7 *The Bacchae* by Euripides has a somewhat bloody ending whereby the hapless hero, Pentheus, is ripped apart by women taking part in a Bacchic rite. One of them is his mother, Agave, who, not recognising her son, displays his decapitated head in triumph. Crassus' starring role is playing Pentheus' head.
8 Arminius, a prince of the Cherusci tribe, had been raised in Rome as a hostage/welcome guest. He'd achieved Roman citizenship and the rank of equestrian. He'd even served with distinction in the Roman army. We have to assume that the entire time he was working his way up in Roman society his heart was black with thoughts of revenge. I think we can agree he did get satisfaction.

9 Modern-day Romania.

10 By the famous general, Agricola, whose successes in Briton earned the jealousy of Domitian, according to Tacitus (who just happens to be Agricola's son-in-law). Domitian was peeved that his own triumph against the Chatti wasn't nearly as impressive as Agricola's.

11 Mention of Domitian's impressive skill as an archer in our sources is actually a dig at him. It suggests he is not a proper manly Roman. It also suggests he has far too much time on his hands.

12 The auxiliary forces were recruited from non-citizen residents of the empire. They are probably local to the area and after having done their twenty-five years' service, will qualify for Roman citizenship. The benefits to the Romans were clear; they pacified the local youth by recruiting them and the army obtained skills, such as archery, that they might not otherwise have.

13 And they described it using the very basest of words, which we shall not repeat here.

14 Which took place during the third Punic War in the second century BCE.

15 In the recent Jewish Wars. When the Romans finally breached the walls, they discovered the enemy had all killed themselves rather than surrender.

16 In the fourth century BCE.

Chapter 11: Religion and Beliefs

1 The emperor's father, Vespasian, joked on his death bed, 'I think I'm turning into a God.' He was absolutely correct in this and everyone soon forgot his somewhat embarrassing death from a bout of violent diarrhoea.

2 Vitellius was overthrown by an army led by Antonius Primus, whose nickname was Beaky. Nobody knows why. Perhaps he had a nose in the shape of a rooster's beak? Perhaps some other part of his anatomy beak-shaped? Perhaps he was overly partial to grain and clucking at first light? It is one of those infuriating mysteries of Roman history that will probably never be solved.

3 The Roman god of the underworld was Pluto who was married to Proserpine.

4 The reason for this ritual, according to Ovid, lies in the story of a boy who caught a fox stealing his family's chickens. Trapping it, he (rather horribly) set it on fire. The blazing fox ran into the farm's corn field and entirely destroyed the crops.

5 The poet Martial presents a huge list of suitable Saturnalia presents *(Epigrams, 13),* including the ones I've listed. Also mentioned are a toothpick, a scarlet cloak, a breast band, a monkey, a dwarf and a sponge.

6 Domitilla died in exile and is considered a martyr by the Christian church, where she is known as Saint Flavia Domitilla.

Chapter 12: Law and Order

1 The Praetorian Guard have a long history of making trouble. It was Praetorian Prefect, Nymphidius Sabinus, who persuaded his guards to abandon Nero and thus hasten that emperor's end. Sabinus, disappointed by Nero's successor, Galba, decided he'd make a better emperor and attempted a coup. Only his guards weren't having it this time and they lynched their own commanding officer, dragging his body through the streets of Rome.

2 Grafitti from Pompeii found in the Street of the Theatres, VIII: 64.

3 Quoted in Mary Beard, *SPQR*, p465.

4 Domitian executed the nephew of Otho (who was emperor for only a few months in 69 CE).

5 Epaphroditus was one of the freedmen with Nero when he died: he'd aided the emperor in his suicide. Epaphroditus had been living quietly for the twenty-five years since Nero's death when Domitian abruptly decided that helping an emperor die was a capital offence. Epaphroditus was exiled and later executed. Presumably as an example to Domitian's own staff so that they would not get any ideas about 'helping' him into suicide.

6 See Claudius' wife, Messalina, who was putting it about all over the place to the extent that she had a second 'marriage' with one of her lovers. When Claudius found out, both of them were executed.

7 The empress Domitia's first husband, Aelius Lamia, made a rather poor joke about the emperor stealing his wife. Domitian stewed on this for fifteen years, before deciding that it was an executable offence.

8 Under Tiberius there was a maelstrom of treason trials and accusations. Some of them, such as the last two in this list, were redefining treason as being vaguely but not purposefully offensive about the emperor. It made for a very paranoid atmosphere.

9 According to Pliny the Younger, the going rate is three denarii a head to buy yourself a decent clapper. *Letters*, 2.14.

10 Pliny the Younger mentions a speech of seven hours.

11 Both Cicero and Domitia's exiles were temporary. They both returned to Rome.

Chapter 13: Politics

1 Rome's first emperor, Augustus, spent a lot of his time claiming he'd restored the Republic and that he was just an ordinary citizen who didn't really instruct the Senate how to govern, nor control every aspect of government. One hundred years later it is clear to all that the Republic has not been restored. However, everyone still insists that Rome doesn't have kings. We'd recommend you don't question this collective delusion.

2 The nomenclator's role is to remember names, so you don't have to. An essential service in any up-and-coming household. He's also very handy at parties.

3 And potentially fatal, remembering that officials and emperors tend to move around with an armed bodyguard by their side.

4 From Plutarch's *Life of Pompey*.

Bibliography

The Penguin Dictionary of Classical Mythology (edited by Stephen Kershaw), (Penguin Books: 1991)

Apicius, *Cookery and Dining in Imperial Rome* (Translated by Joseph Dommers Vehling), (Dover Publications; 1977)

Bauman, Richard A., *Crime & Punishment in Ancient Rome* (Routledge: 1996)

Beard, Mary, *SPQR: A History of Ancient Rome* (Profile Books: 2016)

Beard, Mary, *Pompeii: The Life of a Roman Town* (Profile Books: 2008)

Dickie, Matthew, *Magic and Magicians in The Graeco Roman World* (Routledge: 2001)

Dupont, Florence, *Daily Life in Ancient Rome* (Blackwell: 1992)

Edwards, Catherine, *Death in Ancient Rome* (Yale University Press: 2007)

Galen, *Selected Works* (translated by P.N. Singer), (Oxford University Press: 1997)

Graf, Fritz, *Magic in the Ancient World* (Harvard: 1997)

Hippocratic Writings (translated by Professor Geoffrey Earnest Richard Lloyd) (Penguin Books:1983)

Hopkins, Keith and Mary Beard, *The Colosseum* (Profile: 2005)

Israelowich, Ido, *Patients and Healers in the High Roman Empire* (John Hopkins University Press: 2015).

Juvenal, *The Sixteen Satires* (translated by Peter Green) (Penguin Books: 2004)

Knapp, Robert, *Invisible Romans* (Profile: 2013)

Laes, Christian and Johann Strubbe, *Youth in the Roman Empire: The Young and Restless Years* (CUU: 2014)

Leon, Vicky, *Orgy Planner Wanted: Odd Jobs and Curious Careers in the Ancient World* (Quercus: 2007)

Livy, *Rome and the Mediterranean (translated by Henry Bettenson)* (Penguin Books: 1976)

King, Helen, *Greek and Roman Medicine* (Bristol Classical Press: 2001)

Martial, *The Epigrams* (translated by James Michie) (Penguin Books: 1978)

Matyszak, Philip, *Legionary: The Roman Soldier's Manual* (Thames & Hudson: 2009)

Matyszak, Philip, *Ancient Rome on Five Denarii A Day* (Thames & Hudson: 2007)

Nippel, Winfried, *Public Order in Ancient Rome* (Cambridge University Press: 1985)

Nossov, Konstantin, *Gladiator: Rome's Bloody Spectacle* (Osprey: 2009)

Ovid, *Fasti* (Translated by A.J. Boyle and R.D. Woodard) (Penguin Books: 2004)

Pliny the Elder, *Natural History: A Selection* (translated by John Healey), (Penguin Books: 1991)

Pliny, *The Letters of the Younger Pliny* (translated by Betty Radice) (Penguin Books: 1969)

Plutarch, *Roman Lives* (translated by Robin Waterfield) (Oxford World's Classics: 1999)

Pomeroy, Sarah B, *Goddesses Whores, Wives and Slaves: Women in Classical Antiquity* (Pimlico: 1994)

Scarborough, John, *Roman Medicine* (Camelot Press: 1969)

Seneca, *Letters from a Stoic* (translated by Robin Campbell) (Penguin Books: 2004)

Shelton, Jo-Ann, *As the Romans Did: A Sourcebook in Roman Social History* (Oxford University Press: 1988)

Soranus, *Gynaecology* (Baltimore John Hopkins Press: 1956)

Southern, Pat, *Domitian: Tragic Tyrant* (Routledge: 1997)

Statius, *Complete Works* (Delphi Classics: 2014)

Suetonius, *The Twelve Caesars* (translated by Robert Graves) (Penguin Books: 1989)

Tacitus, *The Annals of Imperial Rome* (translated by Michael Grant) (Penguin Books: 1989)

Tacitus, *The Histories* (translated by Kenneth Wellesley) (Penguin Books: 1995)

Toner, Jerry, *How to Manage your Slaves* (Profile Books: 2015)

Toner, J.P., *Leisure and Ancient Rome* (Blackwells: 1995)

Toynbee J.M.C, *Animals in Roman Life & Art* (Pen & Sword: 2013)

Turcan, Robert, *The Cults of the Roman Empire* (Blackwell: 1996)

Index

of the gens Flavian, xxvii, 97
of Jupiter, Capitoline, xxvii, 94
of Mars Ultor, 45, 127n.8
of Vespasian, 44
of Venus, 45
Theatre, 64
Tiber, river, xiv, 15, 72, 101
Tiberius, emperor, xxxiii, 5, 19
  and expulsion of people from
    Rome, 64, 104
  and Sejanus, xxiii, 44, 121n.20,
    122n.22
  death, 107
  health regime, 57, 69
  execution of relatives,
    xxiii, 96
  laws of, 19, 104, 111, 135n.8
  reign, xxii-xxiii
  relationship with Augustus,
    xxii-xxiii, 15
Time, xxviii-xxx
  time keeping devices, xxx
Titus, emperor, xxxii, 61, 77
  arch of, 44
  baths of, 65
  Judaean campaign, 44, 60,
    122n.23
  opening of Flavian
    amphitheatre, 59-60
  reign xxiv-xxv
  Vesuvius eruption, xxv,
    122n.26
Togas, xxix, 26-7, 29, 33, 99,
  127n.8
  purple striped, 2, 3, 5
Transport, xxvii, xxxi
Triumphs, 33, 89, 133n.10

Urban Cohort, 106-7

Varus, Publius Quinctilius, 88
Vespasian, emperor, 6, 117,
  128n.9
  death, xxiv, 133n.1
  Flavian amphitheatre, 59-60
  family, xxv, xxxii, 14
  Judaean campaign, 122n.25
  omens associated with, 100
  reign, xxiv
  temple of, 44, 97
Vestal Virgins, xiv, 44, 120n.5,
  130n.3
  execution of, 104-5
  legal rights of, 19, 70
Vigiles, 37, 106, 107
Viminal District, xxvii, 107
Violence,
  political, xx, 9, 44, 117-8
  riots, 64, 104
Vitellius, emperor xxiv, 92, 99,
  128n.9, 133n.2
  death, 45
  extravagance of, 5
  gluttony of, 49, 55, 98
Vitruvius, Marcus, 38

Wealth, 5, 7, 32, 47, 127n.2
Wet Nurses, 83
Wine, 14, 51, 56-7, 69, 94,
  120n.3
  as an offering, 97
  and health, 29, 57, 73
Women, xxxiii, 8, 17-20, 65
  childbirth, 18, 68, 94,
    122n.23